Funny FiLL-IN

MY SAFARI ADVENTURE

NATIONAL GEOGRAPHIC
WASHINGTON, D.C.

How to Play Funny Fill-In!

Love to create amazing stories? Good, because this one stars YOU. Get ready to laugh with all your friends—you can play with as many people as you want! Make sure to keep this book on your shelf. You'll want to read it again and again!

Are You Ready to Laugh?

- One person picks a story—you can start at the beginning, the middle, or the end of the book.

- Ask a friend to call out a word that the space asks for—noun, verb, or something else—and write it in the blank space. If there's more than one player, ask the next person to say a word. Extra points for creativity!

- When all the spaces are filled in, you have your very own Funny Fill-In. Read it out loud for a laugh.

- Want to play by yourself? Just fold over the page and use the cardboard insert at the back as a writing pad. Fill in the blank parts of speech list, and copy your answers into the story.

Make sure you check out the amazing **Fun Facts** that appear on every page!

2

To play the game, you'll need to know how to form sentences. This list with examples of the parts of speech and other terms will help you get started:

Noun: The name of a person, place, thing, or idea
Examples: tree, mouth, creature
*The **ocean** is full of colorful **fish**.*

Adjective: A word that describes a noun or pronoun
Examples: green, lazy, friendly
*My **silly** dog won't stop laughing!*

Verb: An action word. In the present tense, a verb often ends in –s or –ing. If the space asks for past tense, changing the vowel or adding a –d or –ed to the end usually will set the sentence in the past.
Examples: swim, hide, plays, running (present tense); biked, rode, jumped (past tense)
*The giraffe **skips** across the savanna.*
*The flower **opened** after the rain.*

Adverb: A word that describes a verb and usually ends in –ly
Examples: quickly, lazily, soundlessly
*Kelley **greedily** ate all the carrots.*

Plural: More than one
Examples: mice, telephones, wrenches
*Why are all the **doors** closing?*

Silly Word or Exclamation: A funny sound, a made-up word, a word you think is totally weird, or a noise someone or something might make
Examples: Ouch! No way! Foozleduzzle! Yikes!
*"**Darn!**" shouted Jim. "These cupcakes are sour!"*

Specific Words: There are many more ways to make your story hilarious. When asked for something like a number, animal, or body part, write in something you think is especially funny.

your name
- noun

time
- noun

noun, plural
- silly word

adjective
- liquid

noun, plural
- noun

noun, plural
- noun, plural

adjective
- verb

adjective
- adjective

noun
- noun

Fun Fact! THE **FIRST EVER** CEREAL BOX PRIZE WAS A **FUNNY BOOK** ABOUT JUNGLE ANIMALS.

WACK-O's

MILK

4

Cereal Sweepstakes

"_Zach_ (your name)! Wake up! It's time to get ready for school!" my mom called up the stairs. I wiped the _Conducter_ (noun) away from my eyes. How was it _8:30_ (time) already? I hopped out of _train_ (noun), threw on my _boots_ (noun, plural), and ran downstairs. I sat down at the table and reached for the _Cochay_ (silly word)-O's, my _Square_ (adjective) cereal. I poured it into a bowl and topped it off with _Oil_ (liquid). Mmmmm. Breakfast of _phones_ (noun, plural)! As I ate, I scanned the back of the box to see if there was a(n) _clock_ (noun) inside. Instead I found this message: "Hey, _juice boxes_ (noun, plural) and _flowers_ (noun, plural)! How'd you like to win a(n) _triangular_ (adjective) African safari? Just _Run_ (verb) out the slip below and mail it to the address on the box. You could be our _great_ (adjective) winner!" I've never won a(n) _black_ (adjective) contest before, but I figured it couldn't hurt to try. I filled out the slip, dropped it in the _stove_ (noun), and caught the _slipper_ (noun) to school.

noun, plural

noun, plural

noun

verb

adjective

color

verb ending in –ing

animal

verb

verb ending in –ed

country

adjective

color

animal

body part

exclamation

noun

verb

Fun Fact! KIDS AS YOUNG AS SEVEN HAVE PILOTED AIRPLANES.

Airplane Escapade

"Buckle your __SEAT BELTS__ and turn off your __boxes__ in preparation for takeoff," the
                noun, plural   noun, plural

flight attendant announced. I had forgotten all about the contest, but just yesterday a(n) __alligator__
                                                                                              noun

arrived telling me to __run__ my bags. I can't believe I'm on a plane to Africa! Mom and Dad
                       verb

were __blue__, too. Mom was dressed head to toe in __black__ safari gear. Next to her, Dad
      adjective   color

was __jumproping__ into a box of crackers and picking out all the __cat__-shaped ones. If you can't
     verb ending in -ing   animal

beat 'em, __hop__ 'em, I figured. So I __defeated__ up and down the aisle pretending I was deep
           verb   verb ending in -ed

in the jungles of __U.S.__ finding __white__ species of animals. In front of me I imagined
                  country   adjective

a(n) __red__ __shark__. It was just what I needed for my collection! Lost in my own fantasy,
     color   animal

I pounced—and accidentally landed on a man's __head__!" __shut up__!" he said. "Sorry!" I
                                              body part   exclamation

replied. I headed back to my __toysrus__. Maybe I should try to __backfire__ for a while.
                             noun   verb

7

country in Africa

exclamation

noun

adjective

clothing item, plural

musical instrument, plural

verb ending in –ing

verb ending in –ing

your last name

color

type of car

adjective ending in –er

noun, plural

noun, plural

noun

adjective

verb

body part

number

Fun Fact! DON'T **EAT** WHILE **WALKING** IN NIGERIA, AFRICA. IT'S THOUGHT TO BE **RUDE!**

The plane touched down on the runway. "Ladies and gentlemen, welcome to _2Bob way_ !" the voice
country in Africa

over the intercom said. " _holerow_ !" I shouted. "I can't believe we're here!" I grabbed my _pillow_
exclamation   _noun_

and headed for the exit. As I walked out, I saw people dressed in _fanncy_ _under pants_
adjective   _clothing item, plural_

playing _flyuts_ , and dancing to the beat. Crowds were _dancing_ and
musical instrument, plural   _verb ending in –ing_

lifting . It looked like so much fun! I pushed through the group and spotted a man holding a sign that
verb ending in –ing

said: " _Moore_ ." "Looks like our ride is here!" Dad said. We followed the driver to a giant _orw ka_
your last name   _color_

corvita . When I climbed in, I saw that the inside was even _penter_ than the outside!
type of car   _adjective ending in –er_

It had two _stars_ , six _rocks_ , and even a(n) _tree_ ! We began the drive to camp.
noun, plural   _noun, plural_   _noun_

The roads were so _sunny_ and bumpy, I thought I might _sing_ , so Dad made me stick my
adjective   _verb_

finger out the window. After about _15_ hour(s), we finally arrived at our destination.
body part   _number_

- silly word
  - adjective
- something big, plural
  - large number
- noun, plural
  - adjective
- room in a house
  - large number
- noun, plural
  - large number
- something expensive, plural
  - favorite drink
- food
  - number
- noun
  - favorite movie
- somewhere awesome
  - body part
- food

Fun Fact! AT A HOTEL IN KENYA, AFRICA, GIRAFFES SOMETIMES STICK THEIR HEADS INTO GUESTS' WINDOWS!

NATIONAL PARK

Roughing It

As we pulled into camp I saw a huge sign that said: "YOU ARE NOW ENTERING _woble_ NATIONAL
silly word

PARK." The driver drove down a road to a group of _blue_ tents the size of _wales_ .
adjective _something big, plural_

He let us out at the biggest one. It was like nothing I've ever seen before! There were _1,000,000_ rooms
large number

and it even had free _ears_ ! I grabbed my bag and ran inside. The huge doorway gave way to a(n)
noun, plural

cool _kitchen_ . This place had everything! There were _1,000,000_ _bags_ and
adjective _room in a house_ _large number_ _noun, plural_

_1,000,000_ _buggatis_ , water fountains that dispensed _snaple_ , and a 24-hour
large number _something expensive, plural_ _favorite drink_

chef who could make me _pasta_ anytime I wanted! In my room there was a(n) _1,000_ -inch flat
food _number_

screen _blanket_ that was already playing my favorite movie: _baywatch_ . This must be what
noun _favorite movie_

beach is like, I thought. Just then, my _leg_ started to rumble. It must be dinner-
somewhere awesome _body part_

time! We went outside and ate traditional African _pizza_ next to a campfire. What an amazing place!
food

past-tense verb

clothing item

body part, plural

greeting

body part, plural

body part, plural

body part, plural

body part

animal

adjective

animal

animal

animal, plural

adjective

noun

adjective

verb ending in –ing

Fun Fact! A HUGE COLONY OF AFRICAN PENGUINS LIVES AT THE TIP OF SOUTH AFRICA.

12

"Rise and shine!" I heard Mom say as I awoke the next morning. It was time for the safari! I _____ (past-tense verb)

out of bed, threw on a clean _____ (clothing item), and brushed my _____ (body part, plural). As I ran outside to join the

group, I saw a great big safari vehicle waiting for us. "Jambo!" our guide said. "That means '_____ (greeting)!'

Please keep your _____ (body part, plural), _____ (body part, plural), and _____ (body part, plural) inside the

vehicle at all times. You wouldn't want to lose a(n) _____ (body part) to a(n) _____ (animal)!"

The ride was loud and bumpy as we drove over _____ (adjective) roads deep into the savanna. Almost

immediately I spotted a(n) _____ (animal), a(n) _____ (animal), and seven _____ (animal, plural). This

was _____ (adjective)! Suddenly the vehicle drove over a huge _____ (noun). Our guide told us to hang

on, it could get a little _____ (adjective). Boy was she right! As I reached for the handle, the vehicle hit

another rock and I went _____ (verb ending in –ing) out the back!

13

- verb ending in –ed
- body part
- adjective
- color
- type of hat
- greeting
- nationality
- exclamation
- adjective
- size
- number
- body part, plural
- nickname
- noun
- body part
- animal

14

When You Meet a Meerkat ...

I must have _kicked_ (verb ending in -ed) my _head_ (body part), because when I came to, I couldn't believe my eyes. There, standing over me, was a(n) _red_ (adjective) _orange_ (color) face wearing a(n) _baseball hat_ (type of hat). I blinked a couple of times, but it was still there. "_hi_ (greeting)." I heard a tiny voice say in a(n) _actors_ (nationality) accent. It was a meerkat! And not just any meerkat, a talking meerkat! He told me that he saw me bounce out of the vehicle, but he must have been the only one, because my ride was gone! "_crap_ (exclamation)!" I said. Now what was I going to do? I was alone in the middle of the _nice_ (adjective) _1,000,000ft_ (size) savanna, where temperatures can reach _10_ (number) degree(s)! The meerkat started to help me to my _legs_ (body part, plural). "Look, _zachattack_ (nickname), it seems like you've taken quite a(n) _giraffe_ (noun) on the _limb_ (body part). How about you come over to my house for breakfast?" I hesitated, but agreed. What else was I going to do? Sit out here as _cat_ (animal) bait?

15

- noun, plural
- noun
- same noun
- large number
- name of animal group
- silly name
- silly name
- silly name
- silly name
- silly name
- large number
- adjective
- clothing item, plural
- insect, plural
- insect, plural
- something gross, plural
- reptile, plural
- exclamation
- adjective

Fun Fact! MEERKATS HAVE BLACK CIRCLES AROUND THEIR EYES THAT LOOK—AND ACT— LIKE SUNGLASSES.

I followed the meerkat into the _____ . "Here we are!" he announced. "_____ sweet
_____(noun, plural)_____   (noun)

_____ ! " I looked around, but saw nothing. Suddenly, I saw something moving in the dirt.
(same noun)

_____ meerkats were popping out of a hole in the ground, one by one! "Meet my _____ ! "
(large number)   (name of animal group)

my new friend said. "This is _____ , _____ , _____ , _____ , and
(silly name)   (silly name)   (silly name)   (silly name)

_____ ... there are _____ others inside. Come on!" I told him I didn't think I would fit. He
(silly name)   (large number)

looked at the tiny opening and then looked back at me. "Right-o, you probably are a little too _____ .
                                                                     (adjective)

That's okay, I'll send breakfast up!" Soon enough, twelve meerkats wearing little _____ lined
                                                                                   (clothing item, plural)

up in front of me. Each one held a tiny tray. One at a time they lifted the tops to reveal _____ ,
                                                                                        (insect, plural)

_____ , _____ _____ , and _____ . " _____ ! No thanks," I said. "I'm not
(insect, plural)   (something gross, plural)   (reptile, plural)   (exclamation)

very hungry." Just then I heard a(n) _____ voice behind me. "You might not be hungry, but I'm starved."
                                       (adjective)

- adverb ending in –ly
  - adjective
- past-tense verb
  - liquid
- adjective
  - adjective
- verb
  - noun
- adjective
  - adjective
- adjective
  - body part
- animal noise ending in –ed
  - body part, plural
- adjective
  - noun
- adjective
  - body part

Fun Fact! ONE ANCIENT EGYPTIAN TEACHER WARNED THAT **VANDALS** WHO HARM HIS TOMB WILL BE **EATEN** BY LIONS!

Scaredy-Cat

_____ I turned around and saw a(n) _____ lioness. I was so scared I
adverb ending in –ly   adjective

almost _____ . Globs of _____ dripped from her _____ teeth. Her
         past-tense verb   liquid   adjective

_____ eyes narrowed in on me. She looked as if she was ready to _____ ! I closed
adjective   verb

my eyes. I thought I was a(n) _____ for sure! But then, instead of feeling _____ claws,
                                noun   adjective

there was something _____ and _____ in my lap. I opened my eyes to see that the
                      adjective   adjective

lioness had her head on my _____ . She licked her paws, _____ _____ like a
                              body part   animal noise ending in –ed

kitten, and asked me to scratch behind her _____ . "I don't eat humans, you see. Too
                                              body part, plural

_____ ," she said. "I was hoping you would share your _____ with me!" I breathed a
adjective   noun

sigh of relief. I told her I was sorry, but I was upset about having lost my _____ group. With that,
                                                                              adjective

she stood up and told me to climb onto her _____ . She was going to help me look!
                                               body part

number

noun

noun

adjective

adjective

color

adjective

animal

animal

year you were born

animal

noun

noun

animal, plural

noun, plural

animal

noun, plural

exclamation

verb

Fun Fact! AFRICAN ELEPHANTS' EARS ARE SHAPED LIKE THE CONTINENT OF AFRICA.

WILD STYLE TOURS

Animal Tourists

For __16,000__ [number] minute(s), I rode on the back of the lioness, clutching her __wine__ [noun]. No sign of the __cat__ [noun] anywhere! But suddenly, in the distance, I saw a(n) __hot__ [adjective] cloud of dust. Could that be them? I wondered. As it approached, I saw the outline of a(n) __healthy__ [adjective] __orange__ [color] elephant, and heard a distinct tour guide voice. "To your left you'll see a(n) __hard__ [adjective] __hamster__ [animal], and to the right please notice a(n) __skunk__ [animal]." I saw that the elephant was carrying several smaller animals on its back and was wearing a sign that said: "WILD STYLE TOURS: BEST PEOPLE WATCHING SINCE __2008__ [year you were born]. NO BITING ALLOWED." Along for the ride there was a(n) __dog__ [animal] with a(n) __toy__ [noun] and __police car__ [noun], two __foxes__ [animal, plural] holding __gates__ [noun, plural], and a(n) __elephant__ [animal] taking __seats__ [noun, plural]. Just then, they spotted me. "__boo__ [exclamation]!" one gasped. Then they all began to __run__ [verb] and yell "HUMAN!" Camera bulbs flashed left and right! The commotion grew louder as the group came closer.

- adjective
  - verb ending in –ing
- verb
  - verb
- verb
  - noun
- adjective
  - something sweet
- adjective
  - adjective
- adjective
  - noun
- past-tense verb
  - past-tense verb
- verb
  - body part
- direction

Humans Can Talk?

"Calm down, everybody!" the tour guide yelled. "Remember the rules. One, humans are very _Smelly_ .
                                                                                    adjective

Absolutely no _Farting_ . Two, if the human gets close to you, _____ immediately and
              verb ending in -ing   verb

_____ . Three, if the human growls at you, _____ and play _____ ." Then I heard
  verb   verb   noun

a(n) _____ cheetah cub asks his mom if he could take me home as a pet. "No, _____ ,"
       adjective   something sweet

the mother replied. "You heard the guide. Humans are _____ ; they make _____ pets."
                                                       adjective   adjective

A(n) _____ snake asked if she could feed me. They all seemed to talk as if I could not understand
       adjective

them. Finally, I spoke up. "Can you help me? I'm looking for my _____ ," I explained. They all
                                                                 noun

_____ and _____ . "I have never heard one talk before," a zebra said. They began asking
past-tense verb   past-tense verb

me questions like how did I _____ on two legs and why did my _____ look like that.
                              verb   body part

Finally, the elephant told me I should head _____ and ask the crocodiles if they had seen my group.
                                              direction

- adjective _____
- number _____
- name of animal group _____
- adjective _____
- noun _____
- past-tense verb _____
- adverb ending in –ly _____
- noun _____
- adjective _____
- sound ending in –ing _____
- number _____
- adjective _____
- verb ending in –ed _____
- exclamation _____
- something gross _____
- animal _____
- favorite card game _____
- verb _____

Fun Fact! MALE LION CUBS STAY WITH THE PRIDE FOR TWO YEARS BEFORE MOM CHASES THEM OFF.

The trip to see the crocodiles was going to be a(n) __siney__ (adjective) one—the river was __7__ (number) mile(s) away! Along the way, the lioness had to stop to tell her __school__ (name of animal group) where she was going. We approached a(n) __luky__ (adjective) __cupcake__ (noun) formation. As she crept closer, she __lived__ (past-tense verb) and told me to wait outside. She did not like the taste of humans, but her family might! I waited __quickly__ (adverb ending in –ly) by a(n) __toys R us__ (noun). Suddenly, I heard a(n) __red__ (adjective) __mooing__ (sound ending in –ing) noise. "Who's there?" I shouted nervously. I turned around to see __65__ (number) __squarc__ (adjective) lion cub(s) spring out from behind a nearby bush. One charged right over and ... __moved__ (verb ending in –ed) me! "__Crap__ (exclamation)!" he said. "You taste like __diarah__ (something gross)!" The cubs sniffed me for a while, then decided they did not want to eat me. Instead, they invited me to play "Pin-the-Tail-on-the-__cat__ (animal)" and __UNO__ (favorite card game). Our games came to an abrupt end when the earth began to __move__ (verb) under our feet. "What's that?" I asked.

past-tense verb

past-tense verb

verb

noun

animal

noun

number

verb ending in –ed

adverb

adjective

past-tense verb

body part

adjective

direction

direction

noun

adjective

verb

EACH YEAR, MORE THAN
ONE MILLION
WILDEBEESTS
MIGRATE FROM TANZANIA
TO KENYA.

Stampede!

"STAMPEDE!" the lion cubs shouted together. I didn't know what to do. I _____studey_____ left, then

I _____carrel_____ right. Rocks were falling all around me. The lion cubs disappeared. I was about

to _____icky_____ up the rock when suddenly I was flung into the _____ball_____ and landed right on the

back of a(n) _____giaraf_____. I didn't know what to do. I was zooming as fast as a(n) _____key_____ on top

of a(n) _____5_____-pound animal! If I fell off, I would be _____saved_____, so I just held on

_____very_____! The animal was clearly _____funny_____. It bucked and _____eight_____,

trying to shake me. Finally, it threw me onto the _____bobe_____ of another one! Then that one threw me,

too! They were clearly having a(n) _____bumpy_____ time, tossing me _____wrst_____ and _____north_____!

Then I saw my opportunity to escape. The _____sun_____ was ahead! If I could just wait until they were closer

I could dive into the _____ichy_____ river. Steady ... I thought. One ... two ... three ... _____ran_____!

exclamation

   adjective

color

   past-tense verb

adjective

   body part

adjective

   color

adjective

   animal, plural

U.S. state

   adjective

adjective

   past-tense verb

past-tense verb

   adverb ending in –ly

verb

Swimming With Crocs

With a(n) "___Shot___!" I landed in the ___bloody orange___ water. I ___wallked___
       exclamation   adjective   color   past-tense verb

on my back trying to figure out what to do. Sure, the crocodiles might know where my family is, but I wasn't

sure I wanted to get ___Juicy___ enough to ask. Suddenly, out of the corner of my ___head___,
                         adjective   body part

I saw a(n) ___fun___ ___blue___ shadow drifting toward me … then it disappeared. "___pretty___
             adjective   color   adjective

___cats___ of ___New york___!" I exclaimed. "What was that?" Then out of nowhere
     animal, plural   U.S. state

a(n) ___hard___ ___soft___ snout rose above me. SPLASH! It crashed down in the water
        adjective   adjective

as I ___clawed___ out of reach. Another figure rose up behind me. I was surrounded by crocodiles!
          past-tense verb

I ___ran___ as it tried to grab me. This must have scared the others, because they seemed to
     past-tense verb

back off ___quickley___. I had to get out of there! At that moment, a huge tail came up beneath
            adverb ending in –ly

me. All it took was one big ___swim___ and I was flying through the air!
                                verb

adjective

adjective

adjective

smelly food, plural

body part, plural

silly name

type of game

large number

clothing item, plural

type of hat, plural

verb

animal

same animal

vegetable, plural

vegetable, plural

favorite snack, plural

favorite candy, plural

favorite dessert, plural

liquid

Fun Fact! A GROUP OF **HIPPOS** IS CALLED A **BLOAT.**

Hungry Hippos

When I opened my eyes everything was _cold_ (adjective). It was _fun_ (adjective) and _anoying_ (adjective) and smelled like rotten _cabbges_ (smelly food, plural). Suddenly, something grabbed me by my _legs_ (body part, plural). I was pulled out of the hole I was stuck in—and staring into the face of a hippo! "Sorry," he said. "You landed right in Uncle _blofn_ (silly name)'s mouth. The kids are playing _fortnite_ (type of game) with his teeth, you see," the hippo said apologetically. "Welcome to our family reunion! Are you hungry?" he asked. I looked around and saw at least _1,000,000_ (large number) hippos. Some were wearing _shirts_ (clothing item, plural) and _colars_ (type of hat, plural) and playing games like "Hide-and-_runing_ (verb)" and "_cat_ (animal), _cat_ (same animal), Goose." Something smelled delicious. I looked around and saw a grill chock-full of _carrots_ (vegetable, plural) and _borife_ (vegetable, plural). There was a table with bowls of _gogert_ (favorite snack, plural), _chocolate_ (favorite candy, plural), and _icecream_ (favorite dessert, plural). And to drink, there was _Snaple_ (liquid). "You're not going to eat me?" I asked. "Course not!" he said. "Hippos are vegetarians!"

adjective

   large number

adjective

   adjective

adjective

   something gross

past-tense verb

   your name

adjective

   adjective

adjective

   color

body part

   silly noise

number

   noun

adjective

Fun Fact! TO AVOID GETTING SUNBURNED, RHINOS WALLOW IN MUD.

Just then I heard a(n) _____ rumbling noise. "Our friends have arrived!" the hippo announced.

adjective

_____ _____ rhinos came into view. They were _____ and _____

large number — adjective — adjective — adjective

and smelled like _____ . I was afraid for a moment, but then one of them _____ at me.

something gross — past-tense verb

"Forgive my manners," the hippo said. "I haven't even introduced you. What's your name?" "_____," I

your name

replied. "And I was wondering if you could help me." I told them my story. When I was finished, a(n) _____

adjective

_____ rhinoceros walked up to me. A(n) _____ _____ tickbird was sitting on his

adjective — adjective — color

_____ . The rhino whispered something I could not hear. But the tickbird must have heard it because it

body part

suddenly flew up and called out a loud "_____ !" _____ other tickbird(s) flew up and joined

silly noise — number

him. They came together in a huddle then broke apart and spelled out words in the sky! It read: "CALLING ALL

BIRDS. NEED HELP. LOST _____ . BE ON THE LOOKOUT FOR _____ VEHICLE."

noun — adjective

- made-up word
  - adjective
- celebrity's name
  - adjective
- adjective
  - large number
- animal, plural
  - large number
- animal, plural
  - large number
- animal, plural
  - animal
- animal
  - pop star
- animal, plural
  - type of game
- animal
  - famous city
- adjective

Fun Fact! A SPOTTED HYENA CAN EAT EVERY PART OF ITS PREY—INCLUDING THE BONES.

African Traffic Jam

I doubted the birdcall would work, but I guessed it couldn't hurt. "Everybody ready to head out?" the hippo asked.

"Where?" I replied. "The safari party at ___MALAWA___ watering hole. It's going to be ___PRETTY___. They say
made-up word · adjective

___JAKE PAUL___ will be there. Climb aboard!" The hippo bent down for me to climb onto his ___BRIGHT___
celebrity's name · adjective

___HURTFUL___ back. I shrugged and pulled myself up. No sooner had we exited the brush than we were stopped dead in
adjective

our tracks. "Traffic jam," the hippo explained. Sure enough, there were ___100 BILLION___ ___PUPPIES___, ___800 BILLION___
large number · animal, plural · large number

___CATS___, and ___30 TRILLION___ ___ELEPHANTS___ all patiently waiting at a standstill. A huge ___GIRAFFE___
animal, plural · large number · animal, plural · animal

and a tiny ___HIPPO___ were groovin' to ___JUSTIN TIMBER___ on safari radio. Two ___MONKEYS___ were playing a
animal · pop star · animal, plural

game of ___TAG___. A(n) ___BEAR___ was reading the ___LA___ _Times_ newspaper. "What's the
type of game · animal · famous city

backup, bub?" the hippo asked a passing giraffe. The giraffe stretched out its ___CUTE___ neck. "Looks like a
adjective

hyena collided with a gazelle. They're exchanging insurance information. We should start moving soon."

WEBCAMS AT **WATERING HOLES** IN AFRICA **ALLOW YOU TO** **WATCH** ANIMALS **24/7.**

adjective

adjective

noun

gymnastics move, plural

type of music

animal

animal

favorite song

baby noise

silly word

silly word

adjective

insect, plural

clothing item, plural

type of dance

The safari party was in full swing when we finally arrived. It was like nothing I had ever seen! We squeezed past

two _____ water buffalo bouncers and made our way in. A(n) _____ gazelle wandered
      adjective   *adjective*

past with a(n) _____ on her head. There were cheetahs doing _____ into the pool.
                noun   *gymnastics move, plural*

A baboon deejay played _____ music, and a limbo line was forming behind two ostriches holding
                        type of music

a snake. There was a lineup of meerkats jumping off a(n) _____ , and a(n) _____ clown
                                                          animal   *animal*

making balloon humans. The party really got going when the deejay started playing " _____ "
                                                                                      favorite song

by Lady _____ and everyone rushed onto the dance floor. Elephants, giraffes, hippos, and rhinos
         baby noise

all joined in to do the _____ hop and the _____ twist. Everyone was getting into the
                        silly word   *silly word*

action! I looked down at my feet and saw two _____ _____ wearing
                                              adjective   *insect, plural*

_____ and dancing the _____ . This was some shindig!
clothing item, plural   *type of dance*

color

> noun

time

> noun

adjective

> adjective ending in –ed

animal

> noun

verb

> noun

noun

> noun, plural

animal, plural

> adjective

animal

> noun, plural

noun

VOLCANOES COULD ONE DAY **SPLIT AFRICA** INTO **TWO** PARTS, AND A NEW **OCEAN** COULD FORM BETWEEN THEM.

Scary Skies

Suddenly everything grew dark. I looked up, and the sky was turning _____ . I checked my
(color)

_____ , but it wasn't even close to _____ yet, and there wasn't a(n) _____
(noun)   (time)   (noun)

in sight. Suddenly I realized thousands of _____ black shapes were filling the sky. The animals
(adjective)

seemed _____ , too. I looked up at the _____ next to me, but he just
(adjective ending in –ed)   (animal)

stared at the _____ . Without warning, someone yelled, " _____ !" and all the animals
(noun)   (verb)

began to run for cover. The crocodiles dove in the _____ , and the ostriches buried their heads in
(noun)

the _____ . The monkeys climbed up into the _____ , and the _____
(noun)   (noun, plural)   (animal, plural)

began to stampede. I had to take cover, fast! I dove under a(n) _____ _____ ,
(adjective)   (animal)

but as it began to move, I decided maybe that wasn't the best idea. Finally, I spotted a table with

_____ and a(n) _____ sitting on it, and I crawled under it.
(noun, plural)   (noun)

- past-tense verb
  - large number
- species of bird
  - species of bird
- species of bird
  - noun, plural
- past-tense verb
  - clothing item
- exclamation
  - adjective
- verb ending in –ing
  - exclamation
- noun
  - body part, plural
- noun
  - type of storm

Fun Fact! A MAN MADE A VIDEO OF HIMSELF **FLYING** WITH HOMEMADE **BIRDS' WINGS**— BUT IT WAS A **FAKE!**

The commotion outside began to die down. I _____ (past-tense verb) my head out to make sure the coast was clear and realized what had been causing all the fuss. There were about _____ (large number) birds circling high in the air. "Looks like your search party is back!" the hippo called to me. With that, a(n) _____ (species of bird), a(n) _____ (species of bird), and a(n) _____ (species of bird) surrounded me. They flapped their _____ (noun, plural) and _____ (past-tense verb), but I couldn't understand them. Without warning, they grabbed me by my _____ (clothing item) and lifted me high into the air. "_____ (exclamation)!" I yelled. "Put me down!" The _____ (adjective) wind was so strong, I could barely open my eyes. I finally managed to look down and saw all of my safari friends below me, _____ (verb ending in –ing) and yelling, "_____ (exclamation)!" It was then I realized the birds must have found my safari group. "Thanks for the _____ (noun)!" I called back. We continued to soar through the air until my _____ (body part, plural) chattered and my _____ (noun) looked like I had been through a(n) _____ (type of storm).

- large number
  - measurement of time, plural
- number
  - adjective ending in –er
- same adjective ending in –er
  - part of a car
- something slow
  - verb ending in –ing
- verb
  - verb
- past-tense verb
  - verb ending in –ing
- exclamation
  - animal sound
- adjective
  - adverb ending in –ly
- verb
  - verb

Fun Fact! WEIGHING UP TO 40 POUNDS (18 KG), AFRICA'S KORI BUSTARD MAY BE THE **HEAVIEST** FLYING ANIMAL.

Dropping In

After what seemed like _____ (large number) _____ (measurement of time, plural), we spotted the safari vehicle. It

must have been going _____ (number) mile(s) per hour! The birds flew _____ (adjective ending in –er) and

_____ (same adjective ending in –er)—that's when I realized they were planning to lower me onto the _____ (part of a car)!

Right then I spotted a(n) _____ (something slow) _____ (verb ending in –ing) on the road up ahead. The

vehicle started to _____ (verb) and _____ (verb) to avoid the collision. Whew! It stopped just in time!

The birds _____ (past-tense verb) me onto the roof of the vehicle. It took a moment to get my balance, but

eventually I was _____ (verb ending in –ing) . "_____ (exclamation)!" I called as the birds flew away.

"_____ (animal sound)!" they called back. Now how on earth was I going to get down? The answer was

obvious, but _____ (adjective). I would have to jump onto the ground. _____ (adverb ending in –ly), I began

to _____ (verb) over to one side. I grabbed hold of the edge. One ... two ... three ... _____ (verb)!

43

- body part
- nickname for mother
- nickname for father
- past-tense verb
- adjective
- large number
- something loud, plural
- adjective
- something large
- body part, plural
- large number
- adjective
- adjective
- adjective
- adjective
- adjective

Fun Fact! DURING ONE SLEEP STAGE, OUR **BODIES** BECOME **PARALYZED** SO WE DON'T ACT OUT OUR **DREAMS.**

The last thing I remember was seeing the ground come closer to my ___leg___ (body part) as I fell to the earth. When I opened my eyes, my parents were standing over me. "___mama___ (nickname for mother)! ___papa___ (nickname for father)! I found you!" I said. They looked at each other and ___jumped___ (past-tense verb). "Found us?" Dad asked. "I didn't know we were missing!" I was ___slinky___ (adjective) and confused. Dad's voice sounded like ___1,000___ (large number) ___songs___ (something loud, plural) and I felt like I had been hit by a(n) ___slimy___ (adjective) ___ocean___ (something large). "How many ___bones___ (body part, plural) am I holding up?" Mom asked. "___5,000___ (large number)," I replied. "Where am I?" I asked. "At camp!" Mom said. "You've been here all day!" "No I haven't!" I said. "I've been out on safari!" I told them about the ___furry___ (adjective) meerkat meal, the ___sexy___ (adjective) stampede, the ___scratchy___ (adjective) hippo reunion, and the ___perky___ (adjective) safari party. "Wow, what a day!" Mom laughed. "That bump on your head must have been more ___lazy___ (adjective) than we thought. You had quite a dream!"

adjective

    adjective

adjective

    noun ending in –ness

type of fruit

    animal, plural

animal, plural

    animal, plural

animal, plural

    type of vegetable

a profession

    animal, plural

food, plural

    past-tense verb

year you were born

    noun

46

Fun Fact! THE WORD "SAFARI" COMES FROM THE SWAHILI WORD FOR "JOURNEY."

The Proof Is in the Picture

It was *not* a dream! There's no way I could have imagined the _butiful_ lioness, or the _good_
adjective ... **adjective**
tour group, or even the _awsome_ crocodiles! My mom must have noticed the look of _blueness_
adjective ... **noun ending in –ness**
on my face, because she said, "Look, _Apple_ , here are the pictures from the safari your dad and I
type of fruit
went on today." I flipped through pictures of _dogs_ and _cats_ . There were even
animal, plural ... **animal, plural**
fishes and _chuwawas_ . Could I be wrong? Maybe my safari adventure really hadn't
animal, plural ... **animal, plural**
happened. "Don't worry, _carrot_ ," my mom said. "The _Sold_ said you'll be able to join us
type of vegetable ... **a profession**
tomorrow." Man, they saw everything and I missed it, I thought. She even had a picture of two _tuRtules_
animal, plural
eating _visps_ . Just then, I noticed a tiny elephant wearing what looked like a sign in the background.
food, plural
I _runnihg_ in as much as I could. And there, in teeny tiny letters, I read: "WILD STYLE TOURS: BEST
past-tense verb
PEOPLE WATCHING SINCE _2008_ ". I smiled to myself and drifted off to _zach_ .
year you were born ... **noun**

47

Credits

Cover, Perseo Medusa/Shutterstock; 4, AnnaIA/Shutterstock; 6, My Good Images/Shutterstock; 8, Galyna Andrushko/Shutterstock; 10, Tupungato/Shutterstock; 12, Chantal de Bruijne/Shutterstock; 14, Graeme Shannon/Shutterstock; 16, Jason Finlay/Shutterstock; 18, Jakub Gruchot/Shutterstock; 20, PHOTOCREO Michal Bednarek/Shutterstock; 22, PHOTOCREO Michal Bednarek/Shutterstock; 24, Totajla/Shutterstock; 26, Stacey Ann Alberts/Shutterstock; 28, Peter Gudella/Shutterstock; 30, Karl W./Shutterstock; 32, Pal Teravagimov/Shutterstock; 34, Isabella Pfenninger/Shutterstock; 36, Lightspring/Shutterstock; 38, Eric Isselée/Shutterstock; 40, Pakhnyushcha/Shutterstock; 42, Oleg Znamenskiy/Shutterstock; 44, Konstantin L./Shutterstock; 46, Dolores Giraldez Alonso/Shutterstock; Trading cards: (UPRT), Golkin Andrey/Dreamstime; (UPLE), Claus Meyer/Minden Pictures/National Geographic Creative; (LORT), Martin Harvey/Kimball Stock; (LOLE), PlusONE/Shutterstock.

Published by the National Geographic Society

Gary E. Knell, *President and Chief Executive Officer*
John M. Fahey, *Chairman of the Board*
Declan Moore, *Executive Vice President; President, Publishing and Travel*
Melina Gerosa Bellows, *Publisher; Chief Creative Officer, Books, Kids, and Family*

Prepared by the Book Division

Hector Sierra, *Senior Vice President and General Manager*
Nancy Laties Feresten, *Senior Vice President, Kids Publishing and Media*
Jennifer Emmett, *Vice President, Editorial Director, Kids Books*
Eva Absher-Schantz, *Design Director, Kids Publishing and Media*
Jay Sumner, *Director of Photography, Kids Publishing*
R. Gary Colbert, *Production Director*
Jennifer A. Thornton, *Director of Managing Editorial*

Staff for This Book

Shelby Alinsky, *Project Editor*
James Hiscott, Jr., *Art Director*
Kelley Miller, *Senior Photo Editor*
Becky Baines, *Writer*
Jason Tharp, *Illustrator*
Ariane Szu-Tu, *Editorial Assistant*
Callie Broaddus, *Design Production Assistant*
Margaret Leist, *Photo Assistant*
Grace Hill, *Associate Managing Editor*
Joan Gossett, *Production Editor*
Lewis R. Bassford, *Production Manager*
Susan Borke, *Legal and Business Affairs*

Production Services

Phillip L. Schlosser, *Senior Vice President*
Chris Brown, *Vice President, NG Book Manufacturing*
Rachel Faulise, *Manager*
Rahsaan Jackson, *Imaging*

Editorial, Design, and Production by Plan B Book Packagers

The National Geographic Society is one of the world's largest nonprofit scientific and educational organizations. Founded in 1888 to "increase and diffuse geographic knowledge," the Society's mission is to inspire people to care about the planet. It reaches more than 400 million people worldwide each month through its official journal, *National Geographic*, and other magazines; National Geographic Channel; television documentaries; music; radio; films; books; DVDs; maps; exhibitions; live events; school publishing programs; interactive media; and merchandise. National Geographic has funded more than 10,000 scientific research, conservation, and exploration projects and supports an education program promoting geographic literacy.

For more information, please call 1-800-NGS LINE (647-5463) or write to the following address:

National Geographic Society, 1145 17th Street N.W.
Washington, D.C. 20036-4688 U.S.A.

Visit us online at nationalgeographic.com/books

For librarians and teachers: ngchildrensbooks.org

More for kids from National Geographic: kids.nationalgeographic.com

For information about special discounts for bulk purchases, please contact National Geographic Books Special Sales: ngspecsales@ngs.org

For rights or permissions inquiries, please contact National Geographic Books Subsidiary Rights: ngbookrights@ngs.org

ISBN: 978-1-4263-1708-8

Printed in China

15/RRDS/1

How to Play Funny Fill-In!

Love to create amazing stories? Good, because this one stars YOU. Get ready to laugh with all your friends—you can play with as many people as you want! Make sure to keep this book on your shelf. You'll want to read it again and again!

Are You Ready to Laugh?

- One person picks a story—you can start at the beginning, the middle, or the end of the book.

- Ask a friend to call out a word that the space asks for—noun, verb, or something else—and write it in the blank space. If there's more than one player, ask the next person to say a word. Extra points for creativity!

- When all the spaces are filled in, you have your very own Funny Fill-In. Read it out loud for a laugh.

- Want to play by yourself? Just fold over the page and use the cardboard insert at the back as a writing pad. Fill in the blank parts of speech list, and copy your answers into the story.

Make sure you check out the amazing **Fun Facts** that appear on every page!

Parts of Speech

To play the game, you'll need to know how to form sentences. This list of the parts of speech and the examples will help you get started:

Noun: The name of a person, place, thing, or idea
Examples: tree, mouth, creature
*The **ocean** is full of colorful **fish**.*

Adjective: A word that describes a noun or pronoun
Examples: green, lazy, friendly
*My **silly** dog won't stop laughing!*

Verb: An action word. In the present tense, a verb usually ends in –s or –ing. If the space asks for past tense, changing the vowel or adding a –d or –ed to the end usually will set the sentence in the past.
Examples: swim, hide, play (present tense);
biked, rode, jumped (past tense)
*The giraffe **skips** across the savanna.*
*The flower **opened** after the rain.*

Adverb: A word that describes a verb and usually ends in –ly
Examples: quickly, lazily, soundlessly
*Kelley **greedily** ate all the carrots.*

Plural: More than one
Examples: mice, telephones, wrenches
*Why are all the **doors** closing?*

Silly Word or Exclamation: A funny sound, a made-up word, a word you think is totally weird, or a noise someone or something might make
Examples: Ouch! No way! Foozleduzzle! Yikes!
*"**Darn!**" shouted Jim. "These cupcakes are sour!"*

Specific Words: There are many more ways to make your story hilarious. When asked for something like a number, animal, or body part, write in something you think is especially funny.

- friend's name
  - celebrity's name
- number
  - verb ending in –ing
- verb ending in –ing
  - noun, plural
- noun, plural
  - animal noise
- same friend
  - animal
- food
  - something gross
- noun
  - noun
- silly word
  - verb ending in –ing

INCOMING MESSAGE

A Message From Space

It was the perfect night for stargazing. _____ and I were lying on the roof of _____
                                       friend's name   celebrity's name

Laboratory, where scientists work as alien hunters. For _____ years, my friend has searched for other
                   number

beings in space. The job involves a lot of _____ and _____ . So tonight, to pass
                    verb ending in –ing   verb ending in –ing

the time, we're watching _____ whiz by overhead and tracing _____ in the sky.
                    noun, plural   noun, plural

In the background, the lab equipment made a(n) _____ sound as it scanned the universe.
                                       animal noise

Just when I asked _____ if the _____ planet was really made of
               same friend   animal

_____ , the sound suddenly got louder. "_____ !" my friend exclaimed.
   food   something gross

This had never happened before, I knew. On the screen of the _____ hooked up to the scanning
                                         noun

_____ was a message. It read: "_____ ! We would like to make contact
   noun   silly word

with another life-form in the universe. Is there anyone out there _____ this message?"
                                         verb ending in –ing

body part, plural

type of candy bar

friend's name

color

verb ending in –s

adverb ending in –ly

noun

relative's name

adjective

your hometown

verb

something enormous

electronic gadget, plural

direction

famous singer

noun

Fun Fact!

ROCKETS
MUST TRAVEL AT LEAST
25,000 MILES
AN HOUR (40,000 KM/H)
TO ESCAPE EARTH'S GRAVITY.

We can't believe our ___LEGS___ . An alien message! "We are located in the ___HERSHEY___
body part, plural   type of candy bar

solar system. Please make contact." Just as ___VINCENT___ and I are about to respond, the screen
friend's name

turns ___blue___ and the computer ___runs___ ! We decide ___QUICKLY___ that we
color   verb ending in –s   adverb ending in –ly

must go on an expedition to this solar system. First things first: We need a(n) ___PERSON___ to fly. And
noun

we need to learn how to fly. ___ANTONIO___ knows where a(n) ___COLORFUL___ ship is parked.
relative's name   adjective

We head to ___W. BABYLON___ , ___JUMP___ inside the ship, and look at the controls.
your hometown   verb

There's a(n) ___MY HEAD___ button, so we press it. The ___drills___
something enormous   electronic gadget, plural

fire up and blast a hole through the wall. The ship moves ___left___ . A voice that sounds like
direction

___LADY GAGA___ begins speaking—it's the ship's onboard robot. We press another ___bug___
famous singer   noun

and rocket into space. There's no turning back now.

- large number
  - noun, plural
- color
  - noun
- verb ending in –ing
  - command
- noun
  - silly word
- food
  - noun
- verb
  - friend's name
- noun
  - something sticky
- something gross
  - body part
- adjective
  - noun
- body part, plural

Fun Fact!

A SPACE SUIT WEIGHS **280 POUNDS** (127 KG) **WITHOUT** AN ASTRONAUT IN IT.

A Wild Spacewalk

We're flying through space at _____ miles per hour in our ship. It's hard to move, but I
                                    large number

manage a quick look outside and see _____ . A(n) _____ _____
                                        noun, plural   color   noun

starts _____ , and the onboard robot warns us: "_____ !" The _____
        verb ending in –ing   command   noun

comes to a dead stop. We're stuck in space! I reach into a box labeled "_____" and pull out
                                                                          silly word

a suit made of _____ . I slip it on, open the _____ and _____
                    food   noun   verb

outside. _____ holds a(n) _____ that's attached to me, so I won't drift away.
            friend's name   noun

I see _____ smeared all over the ship. It must be from flying through the cloud of
        something sticky

_____ . I use my _____ to wipe it off, and suddenly I'm stuck
    something gross   body part

to the ship! Just then, I see a(n) _____ _____ in the distance.
                                    adjective   noun

It's headed right for us! I close my _____ ! "Need help?" a voice says.
                                        body part, plural

9

- friend's name
  - temperature
- foul odor
  - language
- adjective ending in –y
  - silly word
- liquid
  - something soft
- favorite place
  - number
- animal
  - color
- type of bird
  - insect, plural
- type of drink
  - body part, plural
- another body part, plural
  - size
- something gross

Fun Fact!

ASTRONAUTS
DRINK RECYCLED
URINE.

Dinner With an Alien

_____ and I climb aboard the alien spaceship. It's _____ and smells like _____ .
   friend's name   temperature   foul odor

But it's a ride, and we need one—our ship has broken down in space. The alien speaks a little _____ ,
                 language

so we can communicate somewhat. So far, it seems _____ . After traveling for hours, we land
               adjective ending in –y

on the planet _____ . It's raining _____ , and the surface is made of _____ ,
       silly word   liquid   something soft

but otherwise it reminds me of _____ . We head to the alien's house for dinner. There's no table;
         favorite place

instead we eat off the back of a(n) _____ -legged _____ . A(n) _____ _____
         number   animal   color   type of bird

serves us something that looks like _____ swimming in _____ .
         insect, plural   type of drink

We're disgusted, but the alien is scarfing it up—with its _____ !
          body part, plural

We don't want to be rude, so we dig in with our _____ .
         another body part, plural

Dessert is even worse, though: It's a(n) _____ bowl of _____ !
       size   something gross

silly word

    favorite superhero

type of structure

    color

clothing item, plural

    noun, plural

celebrity's name

    shape

another shape

    time

type of pattern

    instrument

verb

    noun

noun

    body part, plural

animal, plural

    favorite song

noun, plural

Fun Fact! ASTRONAUT ALAN SHEPARD HIT THREE **GOLF BALLS** ON THE MOON WHILE EXPLORING ITS SURFACE IN 1971.

WE'RE #3.141

GO π

12

Out-of-This-World Game Day

It's day two on planet _____ , and our alien host wants to take us to watch a game of
                        silly word

_____ . We enter a(n) _____ and see a crowd of aliens.
    favorite superhero   type of structure

This must be a popular sport! The fans are wearing _____ _____ and waving
                                                        color   clothing item, plural

_____ . They chant "_____ !" as the players head onto the field. Half of the
    noun, plural   celebrity's name

players have _____ heads; the other half have _____ heads. At _____ ,
                shape   another shape   time

an alien with _____ skin plays a(n) _____ and the game begins. From what
              type of pattern   instrument

we can tell, the object of the game is to _____ into a(n) _____ while holding a(n)
                                            verb   noun

_____ . When a team scores, the fans slap their _____ together. At halftime,
    noun   body part, plural

a group of _____ comes out and dances to _____ . The team with the
            animal, plural   favorite song

most _____ is declared the winner. The crowd goes wild!
        noun, plural

13

- friend's name
  - silly word
- number
  - your hometown
- noun
  - noun
- something gross
  - scary animal, plural
- large number
  - adjective
- your age
  - noun, plural
- something enormous
  - adjective
- silly word
  - number
- body part, plural
  - verb ending in –s
- singer

14

EAT!

OPEN

MALL

STORES

OVER 5000 STORES

BUY NOW SHOP

OPEN 24 HRS

FREE PARKING

Fun Fact! ASTRONAUT NEIL ARMSTRONG LEFT HIS **SPACE BOOTS** ON THE MOON.

_____ and I have been on planet _____ for _____ weeks now, and we're
friend's name _silly word_ _number_

missing _____ . So we hit the alien mall, in search of _____ and _____ .
your hometown _noun_ _noun_

The first store sells only _____ , so we leave immediately. We pass a pet store full of
something gross

_____ . In another store, we try on a few things, but nothing fits—everything
scary animal, plural

has _____ armholes. By now we're _____ , so we look for the food court. It's easy to
large number _adjective_

find because it's where all the _____ -year-old aliens hang out. After a quick snack of _____ ,
your age _noun, plural_

we get back to shopping. We finally find what we're looking for atop a(n) _____ . Suddenly,
something enormous

a(n) _____ alien appears and says, " _____ ?" We point to what we want
adjective _silly word_

and hold up _____ _____ . The alien _____ away and returns with
number _body part, plural_ _verb ending in –s_

our goods. We pay for them by performing the dance from _____ 's latest video—success!
singer

friend's name

verb ending in –ing

something slippery

silly word

verb

noun

number

body part

adjective ending in –y

verb

same friend

verb

cartoon character

verb

noun

something gross

verb ending in –ing

verb

noun, plural

16

Mind Control

_____ and I are _____ across a field of _____
friend's name   verb ending in –ing   something slippery

on planet _____ . Our alien friend agreed to _____ us here but refused to
          silly word   verb

get out of the _____ after we landed. We're about _____ miles from the ship when
              noun   number

we meet another alien. It holds out its _____ to shake; we grasp it. But we begin to feel
                                        body part

_____ . I suddenly have an overwhelming urge to _____ upside-down,
adjective ending in –y   verb

and _____ starts to _____ backward. Then we start to say, "_____
    same friend   verb   cartoon character

_____ _____ !" over and over. The alien hands us _____ , and we
verb   noun   something gross

start _____ it into our mouths like it's the best thing we've ever eaten. We've lost control
      verb ending in –ing

of ourselves! I reach out and _____ the alien, to try to break its spell. Just then, a beam of
                              verb

_____ hits us. We've been rescued by our alien friend!
noun, plural

17

- verb ending in –ing
  - silly word
- animal, plural
  - animal sound
- verb
  - noun, plural
- friend's name
  - same animal, plural
- shape
  - verb ending in –ing
- something gross
  - feeling
- adjective
  - noun
- same animal
  - noun
- body part
  - verb ending in –s
- food

Fun Fact! CHIMPANZEES, MONKEYS, DOGS, MICE, AND A GUINEA PIG HAVE ALL **JOURNEYED** INTO SPACE.

Animal Planet

I'm on all fours, _____ like an animal. I'm trying to communicate with the inhabitants
                    verb ending in –ing

of planet _____, which is ruled by _____. I start to _____,
          silly word   *animal, plural*   *animal sound*

and the space animals _____ and stick out their _____. I keep up the noise, and
                      verb   *noun, plural*

_____ and the alien who flew us to this planet join in. The _____
friend's name   *same animal, plural*

arrange themselves in a _____ and make a _____ sound. We start to
                        shape   *verb ending in –ing*

copy the sound, and the animals soon offer us a bowl of _____. We don't want
                                                        something gross

to offend them, so we dig in. This makes them _____, and they lead us to the
                                              feeling

_____ _____ where their leader lives. A _____
adjective   *noun*   *same animal*

emerges, wearing a _____ on its _____. It _____
                   noun   *body part*   *verb ending in –s*

a few times, says, "_____," then leaves. We're honored.
                    food

19

color

    adjective

friend's name

    verb

number

    verb

liquid, plural

    shape

noun

    noun

something gross

    color

noun

    large number

body part, plural

    noun, plural

verb ending in –ing

Fun Fact! A **BLACK HOLE,** WHICH HAS THE STRONGEST **GRAVITATIONAL PULL** IN THE UNIVERSE, CAN FORM FROM A SUPERNOVA— THE EXPLOSIVE **DEATH** OF A VERY LARGE STAR.

A Galactic Close Call

We're flying past a(n) _____ hole, and things are getting _____. _____
          color   adjective   friend's name

and I trust our alien pilot, but the holes are known to _____ anything that comes close.
                                                     verb

And we're close—within _____ miles. So we hold tight as the whole ship starts to _____,
               number   verb

and the pilot yells, "Hang on to your _____!" The lights go out, and we start spinning in a
                               liquid, plural

_____. The onboard _____ flies across the ship, colliding with a(n) _____
shape   noun   noun

and spraying _____ everywhere. The lights flicker back on, but flash _____.
               something gross   color

The pilot decides we've got to move faster, so it pulls on the overhead _____ and we increase
                                                     noun

our speed to _____ miles per hour. Our _____ press to the back of
          large number   body part, plural

our seats as we soar through a cloud of _____. We emerge from the other side and
                                      noun, plural

the ship stops _____. We made it!
          verb ending in –ing

- friend's name
  - planet
- noun
  - verb
- noun
  - verb ending in –ing
- verb
  - language
- another planet
  - noun
- noun
  - adjective
- silly word
  - adverb ending in –ly
- room in a house
  - feeling
- same friend
  - type of dance
- large number

Fun Fact!

THE INTERNATIONAL SPACE STATION WEIGHS
861,804 POUNDS
(390,908 KG).

A Visit to the Space Station

Our alien friend has had just about enough of _____ and me. We've had
                                                                (friend's name)

several close calls, so it's dropping us off at the International Space Station, docked above

_____ . The alien presses a(n) _____ in the ship, and we _____
    (planet)   (noun)   (verb)

outside and into a(n) _____ inside the station. Several astronauts _____ aboard it
                            (noun)   (verb ending in –ing)

_____ to our side. In _____ , they ask if we're from _____ . We tell them
    (verb)   (language)   (another planet)

all about our _____ explorations and _____ encounters. They think we're _____ .
                    (noun)   (noun)   (adjective)

So we show them a photo of us with an alien on planet _____ . We're _____
                                                          (silly word)   (adverb ending in –ly)

taken to the _____ to report to the captain. She's _____ and allows
                (room in a house)   (feeling)

_____ and me to stay aboard the station. We quickly settle into zero-gravity life and by the next
    (same friend)

day have already performed _____ _____ times in midair.
                                (type of dance)   (large number)

SCIENTISTS ARE TRACKING
22,000
EARTH-ORBITING
PIECES OF
SPACE JUNK.

friend's name

item of clothing, plural

name of friend's pet

something huge

famous athlete

planet

cartoon character

noun

noun, plural

celebrity's name

another planet

something gross

adjective

year

large number

color

silly word

Galactic Garbage Collectors

To earn our keep aboard the International Space Station, _____ and I sign up for galactic
                                                              friend's name

garbage collection. We report for duty and change into _____ that smell like _____ .
                                                         item of clothing, plural   name of friend's pet

We get into our "truck"—a(n) _____ -size ship powered by _____ . An autopilot
                               something huge   famous athlete

greets us with "Good morning!" before we blast off. Near _____ 's moon, called _____ ,
                                                           planet   cartoon character

we collect our first piece of space junk: an old _____ with _____ sticking out of it.
                                                   noun   noun, plural

Next, we pick up a floating photo of _____ and argue over who gets to keep it. While flying
                                       celebrity's name

past _____ , we scoop up a pile of _____ , and it stinks up the ship. On the
       another planet   something gross

_____ side of the moon, we retrieve a homework assignment written in _____ . We weigh
  adjective   year

the garbage—_____ tons!—before firing it into a(n) _____ hole in the nearby
              large number   color

_____ galaxy. We decide this job definitely doesn't stink.
  silly word

25

adjective ending in –est

    noun, plural

item of clothing

    body part, plural

number

    friend's name

noun

    vegetable, plural

type of bird

    animal

noun

    something lightweight

adjective

    noun, plural

color

    verb ending in –ing

something hot, plural

    noun, plural

verb

26

Fun Fact!

THE FIRST **HUMANLIKE ROBOT** TO TRAVEL INTO SPACE, **ROBOTNAUT 2,** WILL HELP ASTRONAUTS WITH TASKS ON THE INTERNATIONAL SPACE STATION.

Far-Out Gadgets

The International Space Station has all the _____ space gadgets. There are goggles that
                                            adjective ending in –est

let you see _____ that are normally invisible. A special _____ makes
              noun, plural   item of clothing

your _____ disappear within _____ seconds of putting it on.
      body part, plural   number

_____'s personal favorite is a(n) _____ that fires _____
      friend's name   noun   vegetable, plural

when you say, "_____!" One day, while searching for a(n) _____ to fix
                type of bird   animal

a broken _____, I find a pair of glasses. I slip them on and look outside. I see clouds of
            noun

_____ drift by, _____ _____ spinning through space,
something lightweight   adjective   noun, plural

bright _____ rays _____ past. Even the sun looks different: Its surface
         color   verb ending in –ing

is covered in _____, and a halo of _____ surrounds the star.
                something hot, plural   noun, plural

These gadgets _____ you a whole new world—make that a whole new universe!
                verb

27

- noun
  - body part
- color
  - number
- color
  - temperature
- tropical animal, plural
  - body part, plural
- liquid
  - favorite food
- favorite drink
  - large number
- noun, plural
  - something sparkly
- pleasant smell
  - favorite thing, plural
- your name
  - favorite celebrity's name
- famous singer

Fun Fact!

POPULAR ACTIVITIES

ON THE INTERNATIONAL SPACE STATION INCLUDE RACING, DOING SOMERSAULTS AND BACKFLIPS, AND STARING OUT THE WINDOWS AT SPACE.

A Much-Needed Spacecation

It's paradise here on "New Hawaii." It's a welcome vacation after nearly crashing our _____ several
                                                                                          noun

times, visiting other planets, and escaping one _____ -controlling alien. We're lying on a beach
                                                  body part

under a(n) _____ sky and _____ _____ suns that make the planet a perfect _____ .
            color   number   color   temperature

_____ fan us while robots paint our _____ with _____ .
tropical animal, plural   body part, plural   liquid

For meals, we hit the all-you-can-eat buffet stocked with _____ and _____ .
                                                           favorite food   favorite drink

There are _____ -foot-tall _____ to climb; _____ -filled,
           large number   noun, plural   something sparkly

_____ -scented oceans to swim in; and _____ grow on
pleasant smell   favorite thing, plural

trees. Every evening, after the suns set, fireworks spelling out _____ and
                                                                  your name

_____ light up the sky. Every morning, _____
favorite celebrity's name   famous singer

phones our room for our usual wake-up call. I could stay here forever.

29

friend's name

noun

time

type of candy bar

something round

fast animal, plural

weird job

noun, plural

electronic gadget, plural

adjective

verb

something small, plural

noun

large number

something squishy, plural

favorite song

verb

body part, plural

Fun Fact! IF YOU ARE **12 YEARS OLD** ON EARTH, YOU'D BE ABOUT **6 YEARS OLD ON MARS.**

Robots on Mars

Vacation with __VINCENT__ (friend's name) is cut short by a message from the International Space Station:

"Return to the __CAT__ (noun). At __5:31__ (time) you'll train for a special mission to the __HERSHEY__ (type of candy bar) solar system to explore a __CIRCLE__ (something round) for possible colonization." We hop onto our space __BEARS__ (fast animal, plural) and get back to the ship. There, the __DENTIST__ (weird job) gives us our first assignment: Learn to use remote __SPACECRAFTS__ (noun, plural). We're given the __COMPUTERS__ (electronic gadget, plural) that control the Mars rovers and two __COLORFUL__ (adjective) robots that __RUN__ (verb) the planet. Our first day in charge, a giant tornado of __DUDES__ (something small, plural) throws the robots into a deep __SEGWAY__ (noun) populated by aliens with __100__ (large number) heads. Using their teeth made of __SLIMES__ (something squishy, plural), the aliens try to eat the robots. We hit the button labeled "__GAS PEDAL__ (favorite song)," which starts to blare from the robots. The aliens __EXERCISE__ (verb) and cover their __LEGS__ (body part, plural). We guide the rovers and the robots back to safety—saved by a song!

Fun Fact! IN 1908, AN ASTEROID **BLEW UP** IN THE SKY OVER TUNGUSKA, SIBERIA, WITH THE FORCE OF **185 ATOMIC BOMBS.**

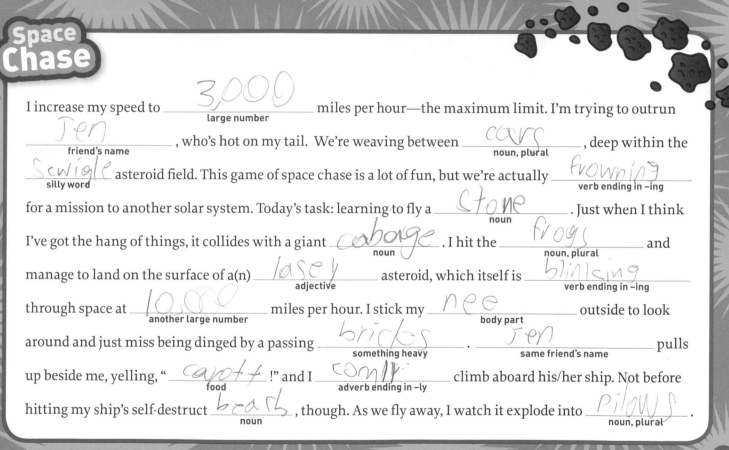

Space Chase

I increase my speed to **3,000** _(large number)_ miles per hour—the maximum limit. I'm trying to outrun **Jen** _(friend's name)_, who's hot on my tail. We're weaving between **cars** _(noun, plural)_, deep within the **scwigle** _(silly word)_ asteroid field. This game of space chase is a lot of fun, but we're actually **frowning** _(verb ending in –ing)_ for a mission to another solar system. Today's task: learning to fly a **stone** _(noun)_. Just when I think I've got the hang of things, it collides with a giant **cabage** _(noun)_. I hit the **frogs** _(noun, plural)_ and manage to land on the surface of a(n) **lasey** _(adjective)_ asteroid, which itself is **blinking** _(verb ending in –ing)_ through space at **10,000** _(another large number)_ miles per hour. I stick my **nee** _(body part)_ outside to look around and just miss being dinged by a passing **bricks** _(something heavy)_. **Jen** _(same friend's name)_ pulls up beside me, yelling, "**carott** _(food)_!" and I **comli** _(adverb ending in –ly)_ climb aboard his/her ship. Not before hitting my ship's self-destruct **beart** _(noun)_, though. As we fly away, I watch it explode into **pilows** _(noun, plural)_.

friend's name

adjective

color

noun

noun, plural

verb

silly word

noun

body part

number

noun, plural

verb

noun

liquid

noun

adjective ending in –y

celebrity's name

Fun Fact! TO BIKE TO THE **MOON** YOU WOULD HAVE TO **PEDAL** NONSTOP FOR ABOUT **3** YEARS.

Moon Mission

__ANTHONY__ (friend's name) and I gasp as the moon— __BRIGHT__ (adjective) and __RED__ (color) —comes into view. It looks like a giant __MAILMAN__ (noun) suspended in space—beautiful. But landing there isn't so great. The surface is littered with __LEGOS__ (noun, plural), which causes our ship to __PLAY EM E__ (verb) and veer off course into a rock. We push the "__QUABGLOB__ (silly word)" button to reverse and accidentally roll into a(n) __CUP__ (noun). I crane my __FOOT__ (body part) out the window to inspect the damage and notice a set of __32__ (number) -toed footprints nearby. We slip into our __ROCKET SHOES__ (noun, plural) and __JUMP EM E__ (verb) out of the ship, excited to follow. The tracks lead us across a giant __PILLOW__ (noun) and around a bubbling pool of __MILK__ (liquid). They come to a stop at a(n) __TV__ (noun). There's writing on it: a space message! __CRAZY__ (adjective ending in -y) with excitement, I lean in close and read aloud the words: "__DRAKE__ (celebrity's name) was here!"

35

- planet
  - food
- friend's name
  - verb ending in –ing
- noun, plural
  - liquid
- noun
  - noun, plural
- adjective ending in –er
  - noun
- something sticky
  - same friend
- noun
  - feeling
- same sticky something
  - noun
- noun
  - same friend
- adjective

36

IN OUR SOLAR SYSTEM **13 PLANETS** ORBIT OUR STAR, THE SUN. SCIENTISTS HAVE IDENTIFIED ABOUT **300 DIFFERENT STARS** AND THEIR ORBITING PLANETS.

Exploring a Gassy Planet

Trying to walk on _____ is like trying to walk on air—impossible! There's no hard surface,
planet

only a swirling mixture of gases that smell like _____ . _____ and I run through them,
food _friend's name_

our final training exercise before _____ another planet in a faraway solar system. In the
verb ending in –ing

haze, we see floating _____ and drops of _____ . A(n) _____ passes by.
noun, plural _liquid_ _noun_

I reach out to collect it, and—poof!—it dissolves into a million _____ . We drift along, the
noun, plural

gases growing _____ . A(n) _____ covered in _____ floats
adjective, ending in –er _noun_ _something sticky_

past, and I grab it. It lifts me up and away, until _____ looks like a tiny _____ .
same friend _noun_

I start to feel _____ , so I lick off the _____ and grab a passing _____ .
feeling _same sticky something_ _noun_

I nab the next _____ that goes by, and it pulls me downward, back to _____ .
noun _same friend_

Reunited, we decide to leave—this planet is too _____ !
adjective

- friend's name
  - silly word
- large number
  - noun, plural
- verb
  - verb ending in –ing
- something scary, plural
  - something stinky
- clothing item
  - body part
- liquid
  - verb
- adverb ending in –ly
  - another body part
- noun
  - noun
- noun
  - adjective
- verb

Fun Fact! ASTRONOMERS CALL AN IDEAL EARTH-LIKE WORLD A "GOLDILOCKS PLANET"— NOT TOO HOT, NOT TOO COLD, BUT JUST RIGHT.

STINK-O-METER

NICE PU

A New Home?

___ADDEN___ and I approach planet ___SUNPINKNUB___, ___55,000___ light-years away in a distant
   friend's name   silly word   large number

solar system. ___BOXES___ at the International Space Station have sent us here to ___RUN___ the
                 noun, plural   verb

planet for possible colonization. So far, it's not looking good. ___PLAYTIME___ ___horrormovies___
                                                                  verb ending in –ing   something scary, plural

that orbit the planet make landing difficult. Immediately after exiting the ship, we notice that the air smells

like ___MOLDY CHEESE___. I pull my ___SWEAT___ over my ___HEAD___ to block
        something stinky   clothing item   body part

the odor. We walk to a nearby river of ___COCA COLA___, and I kneel down and ___JUMP___ it. This is,
                                          liquid   verb

after all, a scientific mission. ___QUICKLY___, I dip in my ___TOE___.
                                  adverb ending in -ly   another body part

Instantly, it turns into a(n) ___MOON___. Freaked out, we run back to the ___PICTURE___.
                               noun   noun

There I eat an emergency space ___lightbulb___ that reverses anything alien.
                                 noun

Then I send an official report: "Planet is ___So very___. Do not ___WALK___ here!"
                                             adjective   verb
                                ___beautiful___

39

- noun, plural
  - number
- color
  - large number
- noun
  - adverb ending in –ly
- verb ending in –ing
  - body part, plural
- something pointy
  - verb
- something slimy
  - another body part, plural
- loud sound
  - verb
- silly word
  - friend's name
- noun, plural
  - verb
- animal, plural

Fun Fact! THE UNIVERSE IS FILLED WITH
VISIBLE LIGHT
AND RADIATION—A KIND OF LIGHT INVISIBLE TO THE NAKED EYE THAT INCLUDES X-RAYS AND RADIO WAVES.

We have to act quickly. According to our _____ , this mystery planet we're on has
                                          noun, plural

only _____ minutes of daylight. Then it's pitch _____ for _____ hours.
      number   *color*   *large number*

As we approach a forest, the_____ _____ sinks below the horizon.
                             noun   *adverb ending in –ly*

Too late—we'll be _____ in total darkness. Our _____ outstretched, we feel
                   verb ending in –ing   *body part, plural*

our way around. It seems this forest isn't made of leaves but rather _____ . Ouch! So we get
                                                                      something pointy

on all fours and _____ ahead. The ground feels like _____ , and it oozes up
                  verb   *something slimy*

between my _____ . Gross! Suddenly, a _____ pierces the silence.
            another body part, plural   *loud sound*

We freeze. Then I feel something _____ me and I scream, "_____ !" But
                                  verb   *silly word*

it's only _____ trying to hand me a pair of night-vision goggles we forgot were in
           friend's name

our _____ . We put them on and _____ like _____ back to the ship.
     noun, plural   *verb*   *animal, plural*

noun, plural

future year

friend's name

number

verb ending in –ing

noun

silly word

your name

verb

noun

body part, plural

noun, plural

food

animal, plural

celebrity's name

noun, plural

verb

verb

PEOPLE REPORT THE MOST **UFO SIGHTINGS** WHEN **VENUS IS CLOSEST TO EARTH.**

Cosmic Twin

I tap the spaceship's _____ (noun, plural) and they flicker to life. The year: _____ (future year). The solar

system: the same one from which _____ (friend's name) and I received an alien message _____ (number)

months ago. We've arrived here by accident, after _____ (verb, ending in –ing) into a giant wormhole. We touch

down on a glowing _____ (noun). There, we get a big surprise: other humans! They greet us by saying,

"_____ (silly word)!" before taking us to their leader. I can't believe who it is—me! Or at least someone who

looks exactly like me. "I'm _____ (your name)," (s)he says. "Did you _____ (verb) my message?" So that's who

sent it—another version of myself living on another _____ (noun). We compare our _____ (body part, plural)

and _____ (noun, plural)—they're exactly alike. We talk for hours about our favorite things— _____ (food),

_____ (animal, plural), and _____ (celebrity's name). We finish each other's _____ (noun, plural). Eventually, it's

time to _____ (verb). I _____ (verb) my cosmic twin goodbye, and we promise to stay in touch.

liquid

electronic gadget

verb ending in –ing

noun

fruit

animal

adjective

noun

adjective

something gross

noun

something sticky

friend's name

noun, plural

something heavy

appliance

clothing item

noun, plural

feeling

Fun Fact! IN 1954, AN EIGHT-POUND (3.6 KG) **METEORITE** CRASHED THROUGH THE ROOF OF AN ALABAMA WOMAN'S HOUSE.

Crash Landing

I've crash-landed before, but this is bad. Our ship is leaking _____ and the _____
                                                                 liquid   electronic gadget

is _____ . Not to mention the _____ is missing; we lost it somewhere over the
   verb ending in – ing   noun

_____ Nebula. All because we swerved to avoid hitting a(n) _____ but instead hit a
   fruit   animal

_____ _____ . Now we've got to use what we find here to fix our ship. We split up. I return
   adjective   noun

with a _____ rock I found in a pile of _____ . It's about the same size
       adjective   something gross

as the ship's busted _____ , so I rip that out and replace it with the rock, using _____
                     noun   something sticky

to hold it in place. _____ returns with _____ , and we use a(n)
                     friend's name   noun, plural

_____ lying nearby to hammer those into the _____ . Last but
   something heavy   appliance

not least, we use an old _____ of mine to plug the ship's leak. We climb
                         clothing item

aboard and fire up the _____ and are _____ when the ship lifts off!
                       noun, plural   feeling

45

- verb
  - friend's name
- adjective
  - verb
- noun, plural
  - animal, plural
- hometown
  - food
- something gross
  - pet
- silly word
  - adjective
- body part
  - animal sound
- teacher's name
  - same friend's name
- item of clothing, plural
  - noun, plural
- favorite song

 ASTRONAUTS WHO RETURNED TO EARTH FROM EARLY MOON MISSIONS WERE QUARANTINED.

I settle our spaceship into Earth's orbit and finally _____ . We made it!
                                                            verb

_____ and I have been on a(n) _____ adventure through the cosmos,
    friend's name   adjective

where I learned how to _____ ; explored _____ ; and met space
                            verb   noun, plural

_____ , aliens, and even another version of myself. It's been awesome, but I'm ready to
    animal, plural

return to _____ . I miss _____ that doesn't/don't taste like _____ . And I miss
              hometown   food   something gross

my _____ , who I can't wait to introduce to my alien pet I've brought back from planet _____ .
        pet   silly word

I reach over and scratch its _____ _____ , and it starts to _____ .
                                  adjective   body part   animal sound

I think I'll name it _____ . _____ and I debate whether our space
                        teacher's name   same friend's name

_____ that let us see invisible _____ will work on Earth. Then it's time
 item of clothing, plural   noun, plural

for our final descent. We turn up _____ and enjoy one last ride.
                                      favorite song

Published by the National Geographic Society

John M. Fahey, *Chairman of the Board and Chief Executive Officer*
Declan Moore, *Executive Vice President; President, Publishing and Travel*
Melina Gerosa Bellows, *Executive Vice President; Chief Creative Officer, Books, Kids, and Family*

Prepared by the Book Division

Hector Sierra, *Senior Vice President and General Manager*
Nancy Laties Feresten, *Senior Vice President, Kids Publishing and Media*
Jay Sumner, *Director of Photography, Children's Publishing*
Jennifer Emmett, *Vice President, Editorial Director, Children's Books*
Eva Absher-Schantz, *Design Director, Kids Publishing and Media*
R. Gary Colbert, *Production Director*
Jennifer A. Thornton, *Director of Managing Editorial*

Staff for This Book

Kate Olesin, *Project Editor*
James Hiscott, Jr., *Art Director*

Kelley Miller, *Senior Photo Editor*
Ruth Ann Thompson, *Designer*
Ariane Szu-Tu, *Editorial Assistant*
Callie Broaddus, *Design Production Assistant*
Hillary Moloney, *Illustrations Assistant*
Emily Krieger, *Writer*
Dan Sipple, *Illustrator*
Grace Hill and Michael O'Connor, *Associate Managing Editors*
Joan Gossett, *Production Editor*
Lewis R. Bassford, *Production Manager*
Susan Borke, *Legal and Business Affairs*
Kayla Klaben, *Intern*
Angela Modany, *Intern*

Manufacturing and Quality Management

Phillip L. Schlosser, *Senior Vice President*
Chris Brown, *Vice President, NG Book Manufacturing*
George Bounelis, *Vice President, Production Services*
Nicole Elliott, *Manager*
Rachel Faulise, *Manager*
Robert L. Barr, *Manager*

The National Geographic Society is one of the world's largest nonprofit scientific and educational organizations. Founded in 1888 to "increase and diffuse geographic knowledge," the Society's mission is to inspire people to care about the planet. It reaches more than 400 million people worldwide each month through its official journal, *National Geographic*, and other magazines; National Geographic Channel; television documentaries; music; radio; films; books; DVDs; maps; exhibitions; live events; school publishing programs; interactive media; and merchandise. National Geographic has funded more than 10,000 scientific research, conservation and exploration projects and supports an education program promoting geographic literacy.

For more information, please call 1-800-NGS LINE (647-5463) or write to the following address:

National Geographic Society, 1145 17th Street N.W., Washington, D.C. 20036-4688 U.S.A.

Visit us online at www.nationalgeographic.com/books

For librarians and teachers: www.ngchildrensbooks.org

More for kids from National Geographic: kids.nationalgeographic.com

For information about special discounts for bulk purchases, please contact National Geographic Books Special Sales: ngspecsales@ngs.org

For rights or permissions inquiries, please contact National Geographic Books Subsidiary Rights: ngbookrights@ngs.org

ISBN: 978-1-4263-1354-7

How to Play Funny Fill-In!

Love to create amazing stories? Good, because this one stars YOU. Get ready to laugh with all your friends—you can play with as many people as you want! Make sure to keep this book on your shelf. You'll want to read it again and again!

Are You Ready to Laugh?

- One person picks a story—you can start at the beginning, the middle, or the end of the book.

- Ask a friend to call out a word that the space asks for—noun, verb, or something else—and write it in the blank space. If there's more than one person, ask the next person to say a word. Extra points for creativity!

- When all the spaces are filled in, you have your very own Funny Fill-In. Read it out loud for a laugh.

- Want to play by yourself? Just fold over the page and use the cardboard insert at the back as a writing pad. Fill in the blank parts of speech list, and copy your answers into the story.

Make sure you check out the amazing **Fun Facts** that appear on every page!

Parts of Speech

To play the game, you'll need to know how to form sentences. This list with examples of the parts of speech and other terms will help you get started:

Noun: The name of a person, place, thing, or idea
> Examples: tree, mouth, creature
> *The **ocean** is full of colorful **fish**.*

Adjective: A word that describes a noun or pronoun
> Examples: green, lazy, friendly
> *My **silly** dog won't stop laughing!*

Verb: An action word. In the present tense, a verb often ends in –s or –ing. If the space asks for past tense, changing the vowel or adding a –d or –ed to the end usually will set the sentence in the past.
> Examples: swim, hide, plays, running (present tense); biked, rode, jumped (past tense)
> *The giraffe **skips** across the savanna.*
> *The flower **opened** after the rain.*

Adverb: A word that describes a verb and usually ends in –ly
> Examples: quickly, lazily, soundlessly
> *Kelley **greedily** ate all the carrots.*

Plural: More than one
> Examples: mice, telephones, wrenches
> *Why are all the **doors** closing?*

Silly Word or Exclamation: A funny sound, a made-up word, a word you think is totally weird, or a noise someone or something might make
> Examples: Ouch! No way! Foozleduzzle! Yikes!
> *"**Darn!**" shouted Jim. "These cupcakes are sour!"*

Specific Words: There are many more ways to make your story hilarious. When asked for something like a number, animal, or body part, write in something you think is especially funny.

- your name
  - your age
- your name
  - number
- country
  - exotic animal
- silly word
  - name beginning with "C"
- relative's name
  - breakfast food
- verb ending in –ing
  - verb ending in –ing
- your name
  - large number
- something small
  - something furry
- something green, plural
  - zodiac sign
- silly word

TOP SECRET

Fun Fact! THE U.S. CENTRAL INTELLIGENCE AGENCY ONCE STRAPPED **CAMERAS ON PIGEONS** TRAINED TO FLY OVER ENEMY TARGETS.

№ AGENT NGK-02

[YOUR NAME]

Agent File

Agent _____ is _____ . (S)he is an asset of the Super Secret Spy Agency currently in training
      your name   *your age*

at the Super Secret Spy Academy. Agent _____ is fluent in _____ languages after growing up
                                        your name   *number*

in several countries, including Kenya, Thailand, Australia, and _____ . Good with animals, the
                                                                  country

agent keeps several exotic pets: Bert, a(n) _____ ; _____ , an iguana; and
                                              exotic animal   *silly word*

_____ , a camel. As a child in Kenya, (s)he had a "pet" giraffe that would stop by for
name beginning with "C"

breakfast every morning. It was named _____ and really loved _____ .
                                        relative's name   *breakfast food*

Agent excels at _____ and _____ . In his/her free time, Agent _____
                verb ending in –ing   *verb ending in –ing*   *your name*

is a speedy reader, and has read over _____ books! Known fears are _____ and
                                        large number   *something small*

_____ . Known allergens are _____ . Agent is a _____ ,
something furry   *something green, plural*   *zodiac sign*

and therefore has traits perfect for a successful spy career. Agent's code name is: _____ .
                                                                                     silly word

board game

sport

noun

body part

noun, plural

noun, plural

noun

letter

adjective

adjective

type of vehicle

something scary

verb ending in –ing

adjective

friend's name

color

shape

school subject

noun, plural

Fun Fact! WASHINGTON, D.C., BECAME THE CAPITAL OF THE UNITED STATES IN 1790. A FRENCH ARTIST AND ENGINEER, PIERRE L'ENFANT, CAREFULLY PLANNED THE CITY.

IN THIS TEMPLE
AS IN THE HEARTS OF THE PE
FOR WHOM HE SAVED THE U
THE MEMORY OF ABRAHAM LII
IS ENSHRINED FOREVER

NOT A SECRET DOOR TO
THE SUPER SECRET SPY ACADEMY

SUPER SECRET SPY ACADE

Super Secret Spy Academy

I was recruited to the Super Secret Spy Academy because I am a _____ master and good at
(board game)

_____ . My school is hidden underneath the Lincoln Memorial in Washington, D.C., and can only
(sport)

be accessed by a secret _____ under Abraham Lincoln's _____ . We have to be careful there
(noun)   (body part)

aren't any _____ watching when we go in! Sometimes I'm late because I have to wait around to
(noun, plural)

blend in with the _____ . I always bring a _____ , just in case. My teacher is Ms. _____ .
(noun, plural)   (noun)   (letter)

She's really _____ , but hates it when we're late. I have a pretty _____ class schedule.
(adjective)   (adjective)

This year I'm taking "Disguise & Camouflage," "_____ Driving," "_____-ology,"
(type of vehicle)   (something scary)

"Code Breaking," and "Stealthy _____ ." My school is _____ because my best
(verb ending in –ing)   (adjective)

friend _____ goes here too. (S)he has _____ hair, _____ glasses, and
(friend's name)   (color)   (shape)

is a _____ genius. When we're not busy learning spy craft, we like to ride our _____ .
(school subject)   (noun, plural)

7

- adjective ending in -est
- adjective
- noun, plural
- size
- adjective
- friend's name
- adverb ending in -ly
- fruit
- same fruit, plural
- noun
- verb
- verb
- something spooky
- country
- number
- same friend's name
- body part
- something sparkly
- noun

Fun Fact! THE LIBRARY OF CONGRESS HAS **838 MILES** (1,349 KM) OF SHELVES FILLED WITH **BOOKS!**

UFO

HOW TO BE A SPY

An Unexpected Mission

My class is on a field trip at the Library of Congress. We've been assigned research papers, so it's lucky that

we are visiting one of the world's _____ libraries. First we get a tour of the building;
                                        adjective ending in –est

it's _____ and very fancy. The shelves are filled with _____ and artifacts. There are
       adjective   _noun, plural_

_____ and _____ books displayed on stands. _____ gets in trouble for trying
 size   _adjective_   _friend's name_

to _____ eat a(n) _____ . "No _____ allowed near the _____ !"
    adverb ending in –ly   _fruit_   _same fruit, plural_   _noun_

yells a librarian. We _____ some books and sit down in a reading room to _____ on
                        verb   _verb_

our papers. Mine is on the _____ history of _____ . After _____
                            something spooky   _country_   _number_

minutes _____ and I are bored out of our _____ and decide to
         same friend's name   _body part_

explore. We see _____ on a _____ in a roped-off
                  something sparkly   _noun_

area with a sign that says: "DO NOT ENTER."

friend's name

   verb

verb

   dance move

verb ending in –ing

   adjective

color

   adverb ending in –ly

verb ending in –ing

   something creepy

verb

   noun

noun, plural

   verb ending in –s

adverb ending in –ly

   verb

adjective

   same friend's name

noise

Fun Fact!

A LINE OF ALL THE **HARRY POTTER BOOKS SOLD** COULD CIRCLE THE EARTH **TWICE.**

10

The Mysterious Man

BEN _(friend's name)_ and I trip _(verb)_ the sign that says "DO NOT ENTER." We skip _(verb)_ over the rope and turk _(dance move)_ into the restricted section. We're having fun laughing _(verb ending in –ing)_ when I notice a(n) grotesque _(adjective)_ man wearing a trench coat and a yellow _(color)_ hat. He's carrying an umbrella and behaving crazily _(adverb ending in –ly)_. My spy senses start stomping _(verb ending in –ing)_. I follow him into a hidden room. He's taking pictures with a camera that looks like a _____ _(something creepy)_! I _____ _(verb)_ him from between a(n) car _(noun)_ and some trees _(noun, plural)_. I'm stealthy, so he doesn't notice me. The man loves _(verb ending in –s)_ books and happily _(adverb ending in –ly)_ throws them on the floor. He's searching for something. When he moves to the next row, I _____ _(verb)_ at one of the _____ _(adjective)_ books he discarded. "HEY, I FOUND YOU!" BEN _(same friend's name)_ shouts, entering the room. The door shuts with a CRASY _(noise)_. I jump up, but the stranger is already gone.

science topic

  verb ending in –s

adjective

  something sharp

verb ending in –ing

  verb ending in –s

something expensive

  noun, plural

something enormous

  exclamation

feeling

  science lab equipment

body part

  adjective

something tiny

  color

item of clothing

The Theft!

At school, during _____ (science topic) class, Ms. B _____ (verb ending in –s) into the room.

She's the _____ (adjective) director of our school and is about as friendly as a(n) _____ (something sharp).

Ms. B tells us that a book was stolen from the Library of Congress while our class was _____ (verb ending in –ing)

there. She _____ (verb ending in –s) that this book is worth more than _____ (something expensive),

because it contains the _____ (noun, plural) to the vault at the Federal Reserve Bank in New York City.

This vault contains enough gold to equal a(n) _____ (something enormous). _____ (exclamation)! I want

to tell Ms. B what I saw, but I'm _____ (feeling) to admit I was in the restricted section. I remove my

_____ (science lab equipment) and shakily raise my _____ (body part). I tell my story about the

_____ (adjective) man in the hat in a voice the size of a(n) _____ (something tiny). "YOU DID WHAT?!"

shouts Ms. B, turning as _____ (color) as her itchy-looking _____ (item of clothing).

13

adjective

    noun, plural

adjective

    color

friend's name (male)

    friend's name (female)

verb ending in –ed

    animal

continent

    noun, plural

item of clothing

    historical figure

color

    adjective

Fun Fact! YOUR EYES PROCESS MORE THAN **120 MILLION** BITS OF INFORMATION EVERY SECOND.

The Mission and a Clue

Two agents arrive at the Academy to help. Agent M is _____ and is wearing dark _____ .

                                             adjective   *noun, plural*

Agent H is very _____ and has vibrant _____ hair, which might be a wig. I look closer and

                           adjective   *color*

realize the agents are _____ and _____ . My friends are real spies!

                               friend's name (male)   *friend's name (female)*

I'm _____ to the case. We return to the scene of the crime—the restricted section

               verb ending in –ed

at the Library of Congress. Books are everywhere, piled as high as a(n) _____ , with titles like

                                                               animal

the *Treasure Map of* _____ . But someone re-shelved all the _____ that were

                              continent   *noun, plural*

on the floor earlier, and there's no sign of the man with the _____ . Discouraged, we leave,

                                                                item of clothing

and we stand outside by a statue of _____ . On the statue's head is a hat—

                                           historical figure

the same _____ one that the _____ man from the library wore! Our first clue!

                 color   *adjective*

- relative's name
  - silly word
- adjective
  - adjective
- liquid
  - number
- type of fruit
  - body part
- verb
  - vehicle
- royal title
  - silly word
- verb
  - electronic gadget
- shape
  - color
- something really old
  - noun

Fun Fact! IN 1900, THE WORLD'S LARGEST CITY WAS LONDON, ENGLAND.

The hat we found at the Library of Congress has a tag that says " __UNCLE RICH__ (relative's name) and __SNICKNURPH__ (silly word)

Purveyor of __COLORFUL__ (adjective) Hats." It's a hat shop in England. So Agent M, Agent H, and I catch a flight to

London to look for a(n) __beautiful__ (adjective) man. We fly first-class, and the attendants bring me __fanta__ (liquid)

perfectly chilled to __85__ (number) degrees. They also bring fresh __GRAPES__ (type of fruit) to put on my

__foot__ (body part) to help me __WALK__ (verb) . I could get used to this! We get off the plane, hop in

a(n) __BLUBCAR__ (vehicle) , and head to Baker Street, the location of the hat shop and home of famous

detective __KNIGHT__ (royal title) __TELETUBBY__ (silly word) . I __SKIP__ (verb) with my __PHONE__ (electronic gadget)

around the store. Near a table filled with _____ (shape) and _____ (color) hats, I see a familiar book.

It looks older than __titanic__ (something really old) . Then I notice a trench coat and umbrella hanging on a

__WINDOW SILL__ (noun) ! The mysterious man must be here!

- verb
  - verb
- adverb ending in –ly
  - color
- something soft
  - sound
- verb ending in –ing
  - body part, plural
- something hard
  - noun
- adjective
  - animal
- item of clothing
  - verb
- adjective
  - adjective
- verb ending in –s
  - adjective
- adjective

Fun Fact! THE ORIGINAL UNIFORMS FOR UMPIRES IN MAJOR LEAGUE BASEBALL INCLUDED TOP HATS!

The Speedy Exit

I know the thief we've been looking for is in this hat shop! I have to _____ the other spies!
                                                                    verb

But I _____ _____ and knock over a rack of _____ and
      verb   adverb ending in –ly   color

_____ hats. It lands with a huge _____ . The shopkeeper comes
something soft   sound

_____ into the room, with the other agents close on his _____ .
verb ending in –ing   body part, plural

Agent H is furious—her stare could cut a(n) _____ . "Please excuse my _____ ,"
                                             something hard   noun

she says. "(S)he's just a very _____ _____ ." Agent M grabs
                                adjective   animal

my _____ and tries to _____ me out of the _____
   item of clothing   verb   adjective

room. But now I see the shopkeeper's _____ face up close. It's him! The thief is the
                                      adjective

shopkeeper! Agent H _____ to the shopkeeper for my _____
                     verb ending in –s   adjective

behavior. We make a(n) _____ exit so we don't blow our cover.
                       adjective

19

- noun
  - verb
- verb
  - noun
- dance move
  - body part, plural
- number
  - noun
- verb
  - noun
- adjective
  - animal print
- color
  - verb ending in –ing
- electronic gadget
  - verb
- small number

Fun Fact! THE LONDON BRIDGE THAT KEPT FALLING DOWN IS NOW IN ARIZONA, IN THE UNITED STATES.

An Unexpected Holiday

I'm in big _____ . The agents won't _____ to me; I almost blew our cover.
          noun   **verb**

But I _____ : "The book thief is the shopkeeper, and he's just down the _____ !"
       verb   **noun**

I _____ to the store. Agent H catches up quickly—she has long _____ .
   dance move   **body part, plural**

We weren't even _____ blocks away, but by the time we get to the shop there's a sign on the front
                number

_____ that says "ON HOLIDAY—Back Next Week." We _____ back through a park.
noun   **verb**

I scan the _____ for the thief. I see a(n) _____ lady wearing _____ pants,
           noun   **adjective**   **animal print**

a crazily patterned shirt, and a(n) _____ striped hat. "I saw you earlier," she says. "The hatmaker's
                                    color

gone to Paris. If you're _____ for him, he was hurrying to the next train." I do a quick
                         verb ending in –ing

check on my spy _____ and confirm that we need to _____ to
                electronic gadget   **verb**

London St. Pancras station. We only have _____ minutes!
                                         small number

- verb
  - color
- noun
  - adjective
- something shiny
  - electronic gadget, plural
- verb ending in –s
  - number
- celebrity
  - verb ending in –s
- adjective
  - direction
- verb
  - speed
- body part
  - verb
- noun
  - silly word
- noun

A VILLAGE IN SOMERSET, ENGLAND, TURNED ITS RED **TELEPHONE BOOTH** INTO A TINY LIBRARY.

TELEPHONE

The Crazy Televator

We're short on time to _____ the train and the thief, but spies always know a shortcut. We reach
                          verb

a(n) _____ phone booth with grimy windows. It looks small from the outside, but when we open
        color

the _____ it's a(n) _____ elevator! It has lots of _____ buttons
        noun   *adjective*   *something shiny*

and weird _____ . Agent M _____ a _____-digit code. Then a light
          electronic gadget, plural   *verb ending in –s*   *number*

turns on and _____ says, "Welcome to the Televator. Destination, please." Agent H
              celebrity

_____ the Televator to St. Pancras train station and we're off! It is not a(n) _____
verb ending in –s   *adjective*

elevator—we go _____ and then _____ right. We must be going _____!
                direction   *verb*   *speed*

I'm dizzy and my _____ hurts; I'm definitely ready to get off the Televator. Finally, we
                  body part

_____ to a stop and the _____ bangs open. We're in the train station with just moments
verb   *noun*

to spare. "_____," the elevator says. We get to the train just as the _____ blows.
            silly word   *noun*

- adjective
  - color
- gemstone, plural
  - noun
- celebrity
  - language
- liquid
  - adjective
- big number
  - adjective
- type of metal
  - number
- vegetable
  - type of seafood
- type of cheese
  - electronic gadget
- flavor
  - type of candy
- favorite food

Fun Fact!

TAKING A TRAIN **1,000 MILES** (1,609 KM) PRODUCES LESS THAN HALF THE **CARBON EMISSIONS** PRODUCED BY TRAVELING THE SAME ROUTE BY PLANE.

Delicious Dining Car

After a run-in with our thief and a(n) _____ Televator ride, I'm starving. So we all head to the
                                        adjective

dining car. It's amazing! The waiters wear _____ uniforms with coordinating _____ .
                                            color   gemstone, plural

Every table has its own chandelier and a personal _____ . Our waiter's name is _____ ,
                                                    noun   celebrity

and (s)he only speaks _____ . I order _____ , but (s)he thinks I want super-_____ size!
                       language   liquid   adjective

(S)he brings us _____ orders. That's far too much, so we share with the _____ tables. Next (s)he
                 big number   adjective

brings a(n) _____ tray of _____ sandwiches. I try a(n) _____ sandwich,
             type of metal   number   vegetable

a(n) _____ sandwich, and a(n) _____ sandwich. I made sure they weren't
      type of seafood   type of cheese

dangerous by testing them with my spy _____ . The dessert trolley comes and we make
                                        electronic gadget

_____ and _____ sundaes. Agent M likes sprinkles on his, I like _____ ,
 flavor   type of candy   favorite food

but Agent H doesn't even like ice cream. We're so full that we go back to our seats and take a nap.

adjective

    adjective

verb

    body part

verb ending in –ing

    adjective

adverb ending in –ly

    verb ending in –ing

number

    type of material

noun

    verb

noun

    verb ending in –ed

color

    type of dog, plural

language

    noun, plural

Fun Fact! THE FIRST MODERN **HIGH-SPEED** TRAIN WAS CALLED THE "BULLET TRAIN."

Caught on the Platform

After our _____ meal and a(n) _____ nap, we arrive at the Gare du Nord in Paris.
adjective   adjective

I really want to _____ my _____. I'm _____ under the
verb   body part   verb ending in –ing

_____ rack, so my head is bent _____. As I'm _____ out of the
adjective   adverb ending in –ly   verb ending in –ing

train, I see him! _____ train cars ahead of us, the book thief is wearing his trench coat and carrying
number

an umbrella and a(n) _____ briefcase. I use my special spy _____ to jump
type of material   noun

over seats and eventually _____ through the _____ of the train. I fall to the platform
verb   noun

and suddenly get _____ in the leashes of two _____ _____.
verb ending in –ed   color   type of dog, plural

Their owner yells at me in _____ until I can get away. The book thief is now gone.
language

But I'm so focused on catching up that I run into a stack of _____ that topples onto
noun, plural

our whole spy team!

- adjective
  - vehicle
- verb
  - adjective
- verb
  - noun
- verb
  - type of appliance
- color
  - item of clothing
- famous painting
  - monument
- type of hat
  - type of bread
- type of cheese
  - something gross
- insect
  - noun

Fun Fact! FRENCH FRIES CAME FROM BELGIUM, NOT FRANCE.

Sightseeing Paris Style

In the _____ terminal, I see the book thief getting in a(n) _____!
          adjective   vehicle

We _____ to catch it, but it drives away. We've lost him. The agents and I call HQ to get
        verb

_____ orders and any new intel. We're told to stay put just in case we _____
  adjective   verb

the thief again. We pass the _____ by sightseeing. We rent bicycles and _____
                                    noun   verb

the city. I have a special _____ that I modify to pedal for me! We stop and Agent M
                              type of appliance

buys a _____ _____. Agent H buys a copy of _____. I buy a
         color   item of clothing   famous painting

keychain of _____ and a _____. We eat a lunch of _____ and
               monument   type of hat   type of bread

_____ in a park. We get _____ too, because it's a French specialty, but I
  type of cheese   something gross

think I'd rather eat a(n) _____. But we're having a blast! We realize we have
                              insect

time to see the main _____—the Eiffel Tower.
                         noun

29

adjective

    verb, past tense

verb

    adjective

big number

    verb

adjective

    verb

adjective

    verb

sport

    animal

noun

    color

verb ending in –ing

    adverb ending in –ly

verb ending in –s

    adjective

adjective

Fun Fact!

SPECIAL SATELLITES **CAN SEE A GRAPEFRUIT** SITTING ON A PICNIC TABLE FROM **250 MILES** (400 KM) ABOVE EARTH.

30

On Top of the Eiffel Tower

The Eiffel Tower is so _____ (adjective). We still haven't heard from Super Secret Spy HQ

or _____ (verb, past tense) the book thief. So we _____ (verb) the stairs to the top. _____ (adjective)

choice; there must be _____ (big number) of them! Once we get to the top, Agent M and Agent H need to

_____ (verb) down because they're _____ (adjective). So I use the spy binoculars to _____ (verb) the view.

The sunset is _____ (adjective), and I watch all the Parisian people _____ (verb) in the grass.

There are children playing _____ (sport), a(n) _____ (animal) with a(n) _____ (noun),

and a man sitting on a _____ (color) bench. Wait! It's the thief we've been _____ (verb ending in –ing) for!

I watch as a woman wearing a beret sits and _____ (adverb ending in –ly) hands him a note. The book thief

_____ (verb ending in –s) the note, crumples it, and drops it into a(n) _____ (adjective) garbage can as he

walks away. I've got to go get it—that note could be _____ (adjective) to our mission!

verb ending in –ing

body part, plural

adjective

verb

spy gadget

verb

something sticky

something blue

adjective

food

store

electronic gadget

sound

verb ending in –s

verb ending in –ing

same electronic gadget

Fun Fact!

A MAN ONCE **RODE A BIKE** DOWN THE EIFFEL TOWER'S **1,665 STEPS.**

The Note and the Code

I'm _____ down the stairs of the Eiffel Tower before the other agents can even get on
              verb ending in –ing

their _____ . I'm fast and _____ , so I can _____ easily through
        body part, plural   adjective   verb

the crowd. But by the time I get to the bench, the book thief and the lady are gone. Agent H uses her

_____ to scan the area, in case they're still nearby. I have to dig to _____ the note
     spy gadget   verb

from the garbage can; it's covered up by _____ , _____ , and
                                            something sticky   something blue

several pieces of _____ _____ . I finally find the note; it's written in code on the
                       adjective   food

back of a(n) _____ receipt. I begin to decipher the code with my _____ .
                 store   electronic gadget

It makes a(n) _____ as it _____ each symbol. Agent M finally arrives,
                  sound   verb ending in –s

huffing and _____ . Just then, the _____ cracks the code! It's an
              verb ending in –ing   same electronic gadget

address, and our next destination is Spain.

33

verb ending in –ing

verb

body part, plural

liquid

noun, plural

vegetable, plural

adjective

body part

verb ending in –s

item of clothing

verb ending in –ing

animal

noun

number

vegetable, plural

verb ending in –ing

something sticky

Fun Fact!

THERE ARE MORE THAN **10,000** KINDS OF TOMATOES. SOME CAN WEIGH MORE THAN **THREE POUNDS** (1.4 KG)!

The agents and I are __running__ _(verb ending in –ing)_ at the open door of an airplane. I'm nervous, but there's no other

way to get out. We jump, __sing__ _(verb)_ our parachute cords, and land on the ground in Buñol, Spain. I look

down and my __butts__ _(body part, plural)_ are in a puddle of red __oil__ _(liquid)_. We need to get across town,

but there are __darts__ _(noun, plural)_ everywhere. And everyone is throwing __cabbages__ _(vegetable, plural)_ at each other!

A(n) __hot__ _(adjective)_ one comes whizzing by and hits Agent M square in the __ball__ _(body part)_. Another

one __jumps__ _(verb ending in –s)_ on my favorite __underwear__ _(item of clothing)_. I learned at Super Secret Spy Academy to

blend in by __hopping__ _(verb ending in –ing)_ like a(n) __manatee__ _(animal)_. I know we'll get across __book__ _(noun)_ faster

if we do that and join the fight. We each grab __1,655__ _(number)_ __carrots__ _(vegetable, plural)_ and start __bouncing__ _(verb ending in –ing)_

and running. Eventually, covered in dripping __goo__ _(something sticky)_, we arrive at our destination.

THE SPORT OF PARKOUR—
MOVING OVER OBSTACLES—
WAS DEVELOPED IN THE
SUBURBS OF PARIS
IN THE 1980s.

- adjective
  - color
- noise
  - noun
- animal
  - adverb ending in –ly
- number
  - noun
- vegetable, plural
  - adjective
- verb ending in –ing
  - noun
- item of clothing, plural
  - something soft, plural
- type of bird, plural
  - verb
- verb
  - noun

Rooftop Chase

At the address from the decoded note, we find a(n) _____ _____ house.
                                                        adjective   color

I hear a(n) _____, and a(n) _____ comes flying off the roof and lands on the street
               noise   noun

in front of us. We look up, and I'm expecting to see a(n) _____, but it's the book thief! He jumps
                                                              animal

_____ from one roof to another and he's quickly getting away. _____ houses down
adverb ending in –ly   number

there's a(n) _____ that I can climb to the roof. I'm still covered in _____
                noun   vegetable, plural

and the roof is _____, so I keep _____ around. I jump to the next
                   adjective   verb ending in –ing

roof and have to grab the _____ so I don't fall off. I run through a clothesline filled with
                              noun

_____ and _____ and lose sight of the thief. Suddenly,
item of clothing, plural   something soft, plural

a flock of _____ flies toward me and I have to _____. When the air
              type of bird, plural   verb

clears, I see the book thief _____ off the roof, down to the _____.
                                verb   noun

verb

    item of clothing

verb

    verb ending in –ing

body part

    adjective

noise

    color

material

    noun, plural

adjective

    verb ending in –s

verb

    verb ending in –s

vehicle

    verb

adjective

    verb

Fun Fact! THE OLDEST RESTAURANT IN THE WORLD IS IN MADRID, SPAIN, AND HAS BEEN OPEN SINCE 1725.

The Book

I'm stuck on the roof. I _____ back to the clothesline, grab a(n) _____ , and use
(verb) (item of clothing)

the power line to _____ down to the street. I'm _____ through the air, out of control,
(verb) (verb ending in –ing)

but I see the thief! I stick my _____ out and trip him; we both crash into a(n) _____
(body part) (adjective)

outdoor café. There's an enormous _____ , and _____ tables and _____
(noise) (color) (material)

_____ go flying. As the thief scrambles to his feet, the _____ book _____
(noun, plural) (adjective) (verb ending in –s)

out of his briefcase. I _____ the book, but the thief _____ through the café. Just then
(verb) (verb ending in –s)

the agents show up in a(n) _____ . They help me up, and we _____ the book together,
(vehicle) (verb)

hoping that the plans are still in it. The pages are _____ and hard to read,
(adjective)

but we _____ the plans to the vault and know that the gold will
(verb)

be safe. Mission accomplished!

39

- number
  - color
- verb
  - verb ending in –ing
- ocean creature, plural
  - flavor
- noun
  - verb
- adverb ending in –ly
  - verb
- something hot
  - something red
- item of clothing
  - something soft
- verb ending in –ing
  - adverb ending in –ly
- verb
  - verb
- vehicle

Fun Fact! THERE ARE SEVEN QUINTILLION, FIVE HUNDRED QUADRILLION GRAINS OF SAND ON EARTH.

Wacky Beach Tan

After all our spy adventures, we're exhausted. Our flight is not for _2_ [number] hours, and we're near the coast, so we decide to hit the beach. The water is a beautiful _blue_ [color] and we _Juping_ [verb] right in. After _walice ing_ [verb ending in -ing] and playing with some _sharks_ [ocean creature, plural], we get some _cholret_ [flavor] ice cream. Well, everyone except for Agent H — she's not a _vincenh_ [noun]. We _raci_ [verb] in the sun and _lyn_ [adverb ending in -ly] become tired. We must have all fallen asleep, because hours later I _swim_ [verb] up. My skin feels like _sun_ [something hot]. I look down and I'm the color of a(n) _sun_ [something red]! I'm sunburnt and have strange lines from my _Brg_ [item of clothing] and _fur_ [something soft]. "Oh no!" shouts Agent H. "We're _fling_ [verb ending in -ing] to miss our flight!" We _autiy_ [adverb ending in -ly] collect our things and _play_ [verb] across the scorching sand. We _Bang_ [verb] into the first _iaMBenaj_ [vehicle] we can find.

THE HUMAN BODY CONTAINS A TINY AMOUNT OF GOLD.

- exclamation
  - small number
- verb
  - vehicle
- color
  - same vehicle
- verb ending in –ing
  - noun
- verb
  - animal
- body part, plural
  - relative's name
- weird job, plural
  - piece of clothing, plural
- body part, plural
  - number
- number
  - verb

The Vault

" _____ ! Our flight is in _____ minutes!" I _____ . "No problem!"
  exclamation   _small number_   _verb_

says our _____ driver. He pushes a _____ button on the dashboard. The _____
         vehicle   _color_   _same vehicle_

takes off, and it feels like we're _____ ! We get to the _____ with time to spare, and
                                   verb ending in –ing   _noun_

_____ all the way home. Per orders from HQ, we must take the book to the vault in New York City
  verb

faster than a(n) _____ . When we get there, a machine scans our _____ before
                 animal   _body part, plural_

we can enter the vault. It's deep underground and smells like _____ . The _____
                                                              relative's name   _weird job, plural_

have to wear special _____ to protect their _____ from the gold.
                     piece of clothing, plural   _body part, plural_

We watch them place the book in the vault with the gold. It takes _____ guards to shut the door, and
                                                                  number

_____ more to _____ the lock. Now that's security every spy can admire!
  number   _verb_

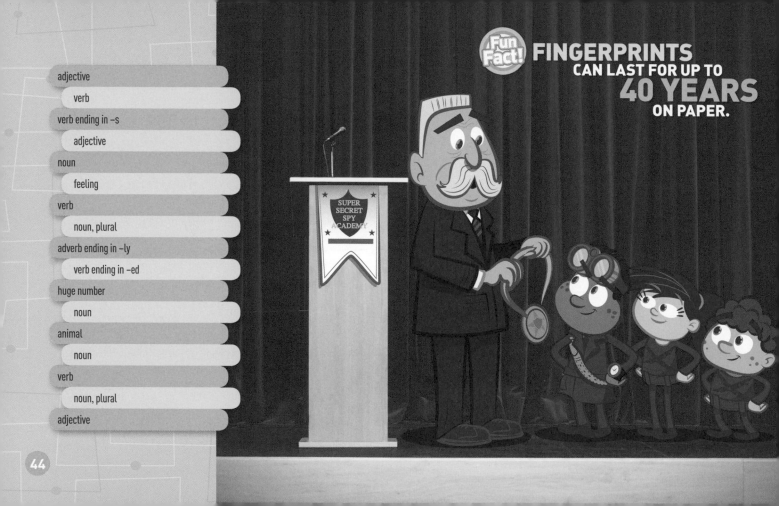

adjective

    verb

verb ending in –s

    adjective

noun

    feeling

verb

    noun, plural

adverb ending in –ly

    verb ending in –ed

huge number

    noun

animal

    noun

verb

    noun, plural

adjective

Fun Fact! FINGERPRINTS CAN LAST FOR UP TO **40 YEARS** ON PAPER.

The Debrief

After ensuring the _____ book is locked safely in the vault, the agents and I _____
                    adjective   verb

back home to Washington, D.C. At the Super Secret Spy HQ, Ms. B debriefs us. She _____ us for
                                                                                  verb ending in –s

a(n) _____ job and tells us that the _____ we brought back will be examined by the
        adjective   noun

_____ team. Already, they _____ that the book thief is none other than the
   feeling   verb

nefarious supervillian J.A.B. The _____ we found will help the agency know more about him.
                                   noun, plural

Most _____ , we _____ his attempt to steal _____ dollars.
      adverb ending in –ly   verb ending in –ed   huge number

The agents and I each have to fill out a pile of _____ taller than a(n) _____ and
                                                   noun   animal

take _____-detector tests. We're given one day to _____ and recover, and then we're
      noun   verb

expected back at our _____ . After returning to the Super Secret Spy Academy, I'm awarded a
                      noun, plural

Gold Star for _____ service.
               adjective

- adjective
  - relative's name
- verb, present tense
  - noun, plural
- famous spy character
  - historical figure
- adjective
  - electronic gadget
- adjective
  - noun, plural
- friend's name
  - type of toy
- noun
  - noun
- noun
  - your name
- noun
  - continent

¡Fun Fact! CAMP PEARY IS THOUGHT TO BE THE SPY SCHOOL FOR THE CIA.

46

My spy adventure was crazy and _____ . I have so many stories to tell _____ .
                                   adjective   relative's name

Sometimes I _____ some small _____ and the stories are even better, just like
              verb, present tense   noun, plural

I'm _____ ! But now that I'm back, I have so much homework to do. I have a paper
      famous spy character

about _____ and a presentation about the _____ benefits of _____ .
        historical figure   adjective   electronic gadget

Besides that, it's _____ to be home and see my family, _____ , and pets. _____
                     adjective   noun, plural   friend's name

just bought a new _____ , so we're learning how to use it. One day after school, I'm
                    type of toy

working in my _____ when my handheld _____ beeps an urgent message. I use my
                 noun   noun

spy _____ to call HQ. Ms. B answers: "Agent _____ , we need your help," she says.
      noun   your name

"Agents H and M will join you. This is an all-hands situation. There are strange _____ signals coming
                                                                                    noun

from _____ , and J.A.B. is still on the loose!" My next mission has just begun!
       continent

Credits

Cover: (RT CTR), Volodymyrkrasyuk/Dreamstime; (UP RT), Cbenjasuwan/Dreamstime; (CTR), Dirk Ercken/Shutterstock; (LO LE), Andrei Shumskiy/Shutterstock; (LO RT), Vitaly Korovin/Shutterstock; 4 (background), Sergiy Serdyuk/Alamy; 4 (RT CTR), Annette Shaff/Shutterstock; 4 (LO RT), LeonP/Shutterstock; 6, fstockfoto/Dreamstime; 8, Lester Lefkowitz/Getty Images; 10, photogl/iStockphoto; 12, Chris Barrett/Hedrich Blessing/Arcaid/Corbis; 14, Pierdelune/iStockphoto; 16, Richard Allen/Alamy; 18, Neil Setchfield/Alamy; 20, I Love Images/Corbis; 22, Peter Crome/Alamy; 24, Sam Tinson/Rex USA; 26, Brotch Images/Alamy; 28, Tomas Marek/Dreamstime; 30, Rodd Halstead/Getty Images; 32, BremecR/iStockphoto; 34, Jasper Juinen/Getty Images; 36, Rtsubin/Dreamstime; 38, Clicks/Getty Images; 40, Gallo Images/Getty Images; 42, Edward J Bock 111/Dreamstime; 44, mbbirdy/iStockphoto; 46, Barbara Helgason/Dreamstime

Published by the National Geographic Society

John M. Fahey, *Chairman of the Board and Chief Executive Officer*

Declan Moore, *Executive Vice President; President, Publishing and Travel*

Melina Gerosa Bellows, *Executive Vice President; Chief Creative Officer, Books, Kids, and Family*

Prepared by the Book Division

Hector Sierra, *Senior Vice President and General Manager*

Nancy Laties Feresten, *Senior Vice President, Kids Publishing and Media*

Jay Sumner, *Director of Photography, Children's Publishing*

Jennifer Emmett, *Vice President, Editorial Director, Children's Books*

Eva Absher-Schantz, *Design Director, Kids Publishing and Media*

R. Gary Colbert, *Production Director*

Jennifer A. Thornton, *Director of Managing Editorial*

Staff for This Book

Kate Olesin, *Project Editor*

James Hiscott Jr., *Art Director*

Kelley Miller, *Senior Photo Editor*

Ruth Ann Thompson, *Designer*

Ariane Szu-Tu, *Editorial Assistant*

Callie Broaddus, *Design Production Assistant*

Margaret Leist, *Illustrations Assistant*

Ruth Musgrave, *Writer*

Jason Tharp, *Illustrator*

Bri Bertoia, *Freelance Photo Editor*

Grace Hill, *Associate Managing Editor*

Joan Gossett, *Production Editor*

Lewis R. Bassford, *Production Manager*

Susan Borke, *Legal and Business Affairs*

Production Services

Phillip L. Schlosser, *Senior Vice President*

Chris Brown, *Vice President, NG Book Manufacturing*

George Bounelis, *Vice President, Production Services*

Nicole Elliott, *Manager*

Rachel Faulise, *Manager*

Robert L. Barr, *Manager*

The National Geographic Society is one of the world's largest nonprofit scientific and educational organizations. Founded in 1888 to "increase and diffuse geographic knowledge," the Society's mission is to inspire people to care about the planet. It reaches more than 400 million people worldwide each month through its official journal, *National Geographic*, and other magazines; National Geographic Channel; television documentaries; music; radio; films; books; DVDs; maps; exhibitions; live events; school publishing programs; interactive media; and merchandise. National Geographic has funded more than 10,000 scientific research, conservation, and exploration projects and supports an education program promoting geographic literacy.

For more information, please call 1-800-NGS LINE (647-5463) or write to the following address:

National Geographic Society, 1145 17th Street N.W., Washington, D.C. 20036-4688 U.S.A.

Visit us online at www.nationalgeographic.com/books

For librarians and teachers: www.ngchildrensbooks.org

More for kids from National Geographic: kids.nationalgeographic.com

For information about special discounts for bulk purchases, please contact National Geographic Books Special Sales: ngspecsales@ngs.org

For rights or permissions inquiries, please contact National Geographic Books Subsidiary Rights: ngbookrights@ngs.org

ISBN: 978-1-4263-1644-9

COLLECT THEM ALL!

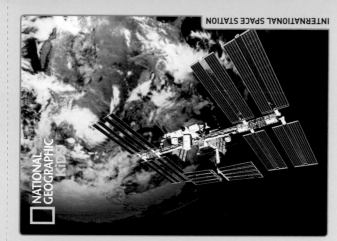

INTERNATIONAL SPACE STATION

NATIONAL GEOGRAPHIC KIDS

MEERKATS

NATIONAL GEOGRAPHIC KIDS

GREEN IGUANA

NATIONAL GEOGRAPHIC KIDS

HIPPOPOTAMUS

NATIONAL GEOGRAPHIC KIDS

International Space Station

FUN FACT

The International Space Station is the biggest object ever flown in space. It floats about 240 miles above Earth's surface. Up to 6 people can live on the spacecraft at one time.

meerkats

FUN FACT

Meerkats are little animals. They are about as tall as four of these cards side by side. Meerkats live in groups called mobs.

green iguana

FUN FACT

This iguana spends most of its time high up in treees. That is where it finds food—leaves, flowers, and fruit.

hippopotamus

FUN FACT

Hippopotamuses spend most of the day in rivers or lakes. This keeps them cool. At night they leave the water to eat grass.